CUNARD

Library

Out of respect for your fellow guests, please return all books as soon as possible. We would also request that books are not taken off the ship as they can easily be damaged by the sun, sea and sand.

Please ensure that books are returned the day before you disembark, failure to do so will incur a charge to your on board account, the same will happen to any damaged books.

The Story *of* Beatrix Potter

The Story *of*
Beatrix Potter

Sarah Gristwood

National Trust

First published in the United Kingdom in 2016 by
National Trust Books
1 Gower Street
London, WC1E 6HD

An imprint of Pavilion Books Company Ltd

Text © Sarah Gristwood, 2016
Volume © National Trust Books, 2016
The National Trust is a registered charity, No. 205846

ISBN: 9781909881808

A CIP catalogue record for this book is available from the British Library.

20 19 18 17 16
10 9 8 7 6 5 4 3 2 1

Printed on PREPS (Publishers' Responsible Environmental Paper Sourcing)
compliant paper.

Reproduction by Mission Productions, Hong Kong
Printed and bound by GPS Group, Slovenia

This book can be ordered direct from the publisher at the website:
www.pavilionbooks.com, or try your local bookshop. Also available at National
Trust shops, including www.nationaltrustbooks.co.uk

Previous page left Beatrix's garden at Hill Top with a spade and rhubarb pots Peter Rabbit might recognise.
Previous page right Benjamin and Peter Rabbit in front of Hill Top, from a greetings card by Beatrix Potter.

Contents

Introduction 6

Part 1: 1866–1900
Beginnings: 'my unloved birthplace' 16
Alarums: 'up one day and down another' 30
Adventures: 'a good summer's work' 42
Experiments: 'a fine fat fungus' 52
Feature: Peter Rabbit 58

Part II: 1900–1913
Acceptance: 'these little books' 62
Sideshows: 'Dear Mr Warne ...' 72
Hill Top: 'something very precious to me' 80
Feature: Pigling Bland 98

Part III: 1913–1943
Mrs Heelis: 'a woman farmer' 102
Community: 'though many changing seasons' 112
Trust: 'a quixotic venture' 126
Endings: 'very far through' 130
Feature: Jemima Puddle-duck and Mrs Tiggy-winkle 130

Afterlife 144
Discovering More 150

Introduction

'A short, round little lady with a smiling rosy face and small bright blue twinkling eyes. I sensed great warmth but at the same time great reserve, even shyness.' That is how a visitor to the village of Near Sawrey, in the Lake District, described Beatrix Potter in the later years of her life. The visitor was Ulla Hyde Parker, whose new-married husband was related to Beatrix's family, and so to Ulla this was not just the creator of Peter Rabbit and Squirrel Nutkin, but also 'Cousin Beatie'.

Beatrix Potter in 1936 with her two Pekingese, Chuleh and Tzusee.

'She wore a thick brown tweed skirt of natural colour and a heavy knitted jersey, strong leather shoes and one could just glimpse the hand-knitted woollen stocking beneath her long, somewhat full skirt,' Ulla recalled. 'A small black straw hat was held in place by a piece of elastic under the chin, just like a child would wear.' Later in the day, the straw hat was replaced by a white muslin mob cap – rheumatic fever in her girlhood had left Beatrix with a small bald patch. Another who visited in these years, the artist Josefina de Vasconcellos, was startled to find her wearing on her head a knitted tea cosy.

Beatrix and Ulla became friends, although 'she did not invite friendships... She was always kind but closed up, and what lay behind other people's exteriors did not seem to interest her.' But one day, Cousin Beatie said: 'Come, I have something to show you, something very precious to me.' The two walked through the heavy summer's dew, through the meadow which lies below Castle Cottage, the house where Beatrix and her husband William Heelis spent all of their married life. Through the gate featured in *The Tale of Tom Kitten*, and up the narrow path between the fragrant flower beds to the door of the house at Hill Top farm.

'We reached the front door,' Ulla recalled, 'and as she placed the key in its lock she said, "It is in here I go to be quiet and still with myself." I looked into the old front-room-cum-kitchen, completely furnished, every tiny item in its place. "This is me," or words to that effect, she added, "the deepest me, the part one has to be alone with. So you see, when Cousin Willie asked me to marry him I said yes, but I also said we

The entrance hall at Hill Top doubles as a kitchen, with a stone-flagged floor and kitchen range identical to the one illustrated in *The Tale of Samuel Whiskers*. Paper covers the ceiling as well as the walls, and a collection of horse-brasses hangs above the fireplace.

From their earliest years Beatrix and her brother Bertram made collections of natural objects.

cannot live here at Hill Top. We will live at Castle Cottage, as I must leave everything here as it is. So after I married I just locked the door and left.'

As Ulla walked in – through the hall and into the front parlour – the old house looked as if someone still lived there, 'except that the dust lay like a fine grey veil over everything'. Cobwebs hung in the corners, above the 'faded floral carpet, the little upholstered chairs covered in faded flowered chintz'. The cobwebs and the dust are now long gone, with the house in the care of the National Trust. Just seventy years since it first opened to the public, Hill Top is a place of pilgrimage for many thousands of visitors today. But everything else in Beatrix's sanctuary remains just as she wanted it.

'Whenever I opened drawers and chests they were packed with wonderful things. One drawer had the most lovely old dolls in it,' Ulla recalled. When World War II came, Beatrix let Ulla and her family stay at Hill Top, when Ulla's husband need peace and quiet after a dreadful injury. Beatrix told them they were the first people to sleep in 'Tom Kitten's house' since she herself had left.

In the last summer of Beatrix's life, she spent hours arranging her treasures here – the china ('I am conceited about arranging china'), the quilts, the curios. A square piano and the family Bible, her grandmother's warming pan, and a nit comb made for the dolls. Tiny bronze figures of characters from her books, pieces of her own embroidery, and the old oak furniture she used to collect from sales around the area. A doll's house with the very plaster plates of food which Tom Thumb and Hunca Munca stole in *The Tale of Two Bad Mice*; and a huge seventeenth-century oil painting of Noah and the flood. The National Trust staff found dozens of little notes stuck on

Right The collection of curios Beatrix cherished at Hill Top range from bead bags to bronze figures of the characters she created. 'I have taken much pleasure in collecting some oddments,' she wrote modestly.

the back of Beatrix's treasures, detailing how she came by each item, and often the price that she had paid.

Some of the things are valuable in themselves, some only because her work – her fame – has made them so. Beatrix once expressed her puzzlement that more people did not love and value the simple ordinary old things of everyday life. 'It is extraordinary how little people value old things if they are of little intrinsic value.'

Left The view from the New Room at Hill Top, where Beatrix did her writing.
Above In the New Room, Beatrix wrote surrounded by great landscapes created by her painter brother Bertram. She collected old oak furniture like this early eighteenth century bureau.

House leeks cling to the roofs and ledges at Hill Top.

But if this is the home of an artist – and, on old oak furniture, an expert – it is also the secret treasure trove of (as Beatrix described herself once) a child who 'never grew up'. Hill Top, Beatrix wrote, was a funny old house, that 'would amuse children very much'. Thick walls, with rats' nests and a child's clay marbles hidden in the gap between the two faces of stone. 'I never saw such a place for hide & seek.'

She described Hill Top in an unpublished but amazingly detailed piece intended for the volume *The Fairy Caravan*, which she put together late in life for her American admirers. It was considered too personal to be published in her own country. 'It is a good, dry, sound old house. It has stood a many hundred years and may stand as many more.'

She wrote of the flowers which 'love the house, they try to come in . . . The golden-flowered great St. John's wort pushes up between the flags in the porch and has peeped up between the skirting and the flags in the hall-place before now, and the old lilac that blew down had its roots under the parlour floor when they lifted up the boards. House-leek grows on the window-sills and ledges. Clematis chokes the spouts.'

In the garden is the rhubarb patch where Jemima Puddle-duck laid her eggs. Soft fruits and herbs tussle for space with the flowers – wallflowers and cabbage-roses, blue gentian and red japonica-quince. The phlox would be followed by Michaelmas daisies and chrysanthemums, and a wilderness of snowdrops after winter came. Beatrix wrote, too, with love in every line, of the brass turning-spit and coal-scuttle inside the house, the 'cupboards and cupboards' and the bookroom over the porch with its 'dusty parchment smell'.

In that small room, Ulla Hyde Parker found a desk, and inside it, when she lifted the top, 'pages and pages written in the strangest and quite incomprehensible script. I wondered what on earth it could be.' Later, Ulla realised it must have been the secret, coded, diary Beatrix Potter wrote from her teens until she was 30. The publication of the diary played an important role in the celebrations which, in 1966, marked the 100th anniversary of Beatrix Potter's birth. Perhaps it and the letters she wrote helped show a Beatrix whose 'Little Books' could have a fresh charm even for the 'Swinging Sixties' – and, now, for our own day.

150 years after her birth, not only are the characters she created still legends, but large tracts of the Lake District are still preserved for us through Beatrix Potter's care. Iconic names, like Tarn Hows and Troutbeck. But it is in this unassuming house that her spirit lives most visibly – the spirit of the woman Josefina de Vasconcellos described, rolling a little as she laughed, slapping her small chubby hands on her knee. Josefina saw her as one of her own little animal characters and Beatrix, sketching herself as Mrs Tiggy-winkle, seemed to agree. The animals too seem to inhabit the house where she pictured them – Tabitha Twitchit seeing her family off from the porch, Samuel Whiskers at the top of the stairway.

'It's a pretty old place, and I have taken much pleasure collecting some oddments, hoping that some day the National Trust might care to preserve it along with my land,' wrote Beatrix modestly. To countless visitors it has seemed, instead, a gateway into her world – and, 150 years after her birth, one that still welcomes us today.

The garden at Hill Top. Beatrix wrote of how she loved 'a regular old-fashioned farm garden, with a box hedge round the flower bed, and moss roses and pansies and black currants and strawberries and peas'. Tom Kitten and his sisters can be seen walking down this path.

Part I

1866–1900

Beginnings: 'my unloved birthplace'

On Saturday 28 June 1866 – so *The Times* announced – the wife of Rupert Potter Esq, barrister-at-law, of Bolton Gardens in London, was delivered of a daughter – Helen Beatrix, known in her family as 'Bee'.

2, Bolton Gardens was a prosperous place, and the nursery on the third floor of the tall house looked towards the new museums of South Kensington. A solid new-build, with a garden to the front and rear, it was the kind that would appeal to a couple from the successful professional or mercantile classes.

Near the end of her life, hearing the house had been destroyed by a World War II bomb, Beatrix would call it her 'unloved birthplace', and she would remember hers as an 'unhappy home circle'. The environment in which she was raised was indeed repressive to our eyes. But a measure of repression was the norm for a Victorian girl of the moneyed classes, and Beatrix's upbringing did afford her some unusual opportunities. The source of her particular distress may have been two-fold.

The first problem was just how long she would be called on to endure life as a daughter at home. Beatrix was born at a time when Victoria's reign had still more than half its span to run. (She herself remembered the death 'of an old French soldier who had been in the Battle of Waterloo'.) Beatrix would not begin to publish her books until the start of the next century; she would

Beatrix Potter (left, aged 5) holding a toy rabbit, with her cousin Alice Crompton Potter, taken by her father Rupert Potter, c. 1871.

not marry until the eve of World War One. For almost half a century, then, Bolton Gardens would be her principal home.

The other problem, of course, was that Beatrix's heart was always in the country. 'It sometimes happens, that the town child is more alive to the fresh beauty of the country than a child who is country born. My brother and I were born in London because my father was a lawyer there,' said Beatrix Potter many years later. 'But our descent – our interest and our joy was in the north country.' Indeed it was from the north country that the family sprang. 'I am descended from generations of Lancashire yeomen and weavers; obstinate, hard-headed, matter-of-fact folk … As far back as I can go they were Puritans, Nonjurors, Nonconformists, Dissenters.' People, she added, who probably rather enjoyed any persecution they suffered for their faith. Beatrix's parents were Unitarians, their beliefs and their social practices (the Potters did not celebrate Christmas) often different from those of the Anglican church. Beatrix might benefit, in the years ahead, from the freer thought of the Dissenting

In 1889 Beatrix's father Rupert photographed the houses at Bolton Garden in South Kensington, where Beatrix was born, and which remained her home for some forty years. But when the Potter's house was destroyed by a bomb during World War II, Beatrix had no regrets.

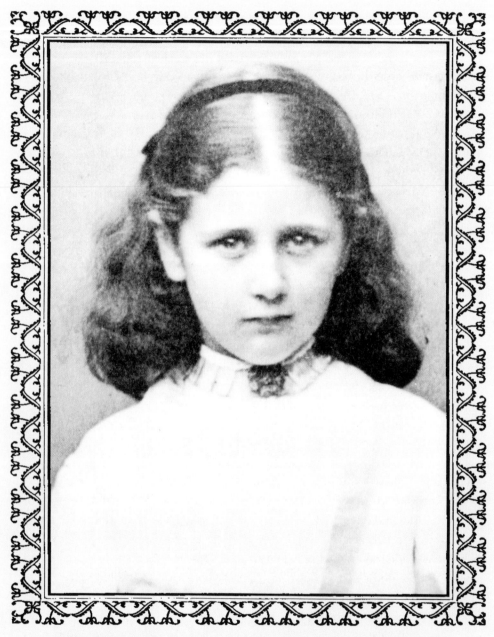

Beatrix at nine was a beautiful child, much photographed by her father Rupert, and admired by his artist friends, who included the painter Sir John Everett Millais, the creator of 'Bubbles'.

networks, but in another sense their difference curtailed the social life the well-to-do Potters might otherwise have enjoyed.

Beatrix's grandfather Edmund Potter had been owner of a large calico printing works near Manchester – a resourceful, enlightened employer, President of the Chamber of Commerce, eventually elected Liberal Member of Parliament for Carlisle. His duties in Parliament had brought him south, and in the year of Beatrix's birth he purchased Camfield Place in Essendon, Hertfordshire. Here Beatrix would become particularly attached to his wife, her grandmother, once the beautiful Jessie Crompton. Jessie's father too had owned property in Lancashire and the Lake District – an eighteenth-century Crompton had even got caught up in the Jacobite rebellion – and it may have been he of whom Beatrix was thinking when she wrote in later life that 'a strongly marked personality can influence descendants for generations'. She was, she said, 'a believer in breed'.

Beatrix's mother Helen came likewise of Manchester cotton-trade stock and Beatrix remembers her maternal grandmother, Grandma Leech, telling her about coming to London on the stagecoach. Grandma Leech sounds to have been another lively woman. The young Beatrix noted, from her grandmother's stories, that 'crinolines seem to have been a great trouble, particularly on tours abroad … It was almost impossible to ride a mule with one on.' But little of this made its way through to Helen Potter, Beatrix's mother, who from anything her daughter said or hinted survives only as a repressive influence in her life.

For the immediate world of Beatrix's childhood was the constricting world of Victorian childhood – a world of calling cards and cutlets, of hairbands whose elastic cut into her skin and of carefully selected outings. This was the world from which she would flee to Hill Top. It was a lonely childhood where companions – human companions – of her own age were concerned. Ulla Hyde Parker would notice how 'she who understood so well how to stir a child's imagination seemed rather shy of them … Not only had she no children of her own; she told me that when she was a child she was not allowed to meet or mix with other children.' Beatrix's mother was afraid they would 'catch germs'. Still, March 1872 saw the birth of a younger brother Bertram (or, officially, Walter Bertram). He would be her friend and ally – later she would speak of the two of them as 'a mutual admiration society'.

Beatrix grew up in a golden age of children's literature, and particularly of Illustration. Aged 6 or 7 she was given a copy of Lewis Carroll's *Alice's Adventures in Wonderland*, and immediately became 'absorbed' in the Tenniel illustrations.

In some ways, as Beatrix herself would acknowledge, that very isolation may have fostered her imagination. 'Thank goodness, my education was neglected; I was never sent to school,' she wrote later in life – 'it would have rubbed off some of the originality (if I had not died of shyness or been killed with over pressure). I fancy I could have been taught anything if I had been caught young; but it was in the days when parents kept governesses, and only boys went to school in most families.' So Beatrix had indeed a governess, who gave her the usual accomplishments and a good grounding in languages. She would be able to critique the translations of her books with some authority. But perhaps her truest education lay elsewhere.

For there were, you might say, cracks in the carefully plastered façade of Bolton Gardens – spaces that would allow Beatrix's imagination to run free. One of the earliest came from her nurse, a Scot, from whom she heard of 'witches, fairies and the creed of the terrible John Calvin (the creed rubbed off but the fairies remained)'.

'I do not remember a time when I did not try to invent pictures and make for myself a fairyland,' she later wrote, 'amongst the wild flowers, the animals, fungi, mosses, woods and stream, all the thousand objects of the countryside; that pleasant unchanging world of realism and romance, which in our northern clime is stiffened by hard weather, a tough ancestry, and the strength that comes from the hills.'

Beatrix grew up surrounded by books, with the wonderful illustrations of the late-Victorian age. *Aesop's Fables*, *The Water-Babies* (as well as the obvious Bible and *Pilgrim's Progress*), Edward Lear's *Book of Nonsense* and the Lewis Carroll's *Alice's Adventures in Wonderland* as illustrated by Tenniel – besides what she could find in the family library. She would learn to read, she claimed later, on Sir Walter Scott's Waverley novels. She would also be deeply familiar with the illustrations of Randolph Caldecott, which her father collected and which she set out to copy.

Beatrix was only four when she was given Edward Lear's *Book of Nonsense*. Later in life Lear's 'Owl and the Pussy-Cat' would influence her own writing – notably *The Tale of Little Pig Robinson* (1930) – and she made her own illustrations for several of his rhymes.

A set of plates transfer-painted by Rupert Potter hangs in the entrance hall at Hill Top. Like his daughter, he was a close observer of the natural world.

The Potters, what's more, moved in imaginative circles. The Pre-Raphaelite painter John Everett Millais was a friend of Beatrix's father, and his teasing often used to bring a blush to her cheeks. Rupert Potter was a keen and expert amateur photographer who frequently photographed sitters or landscapes for Millais' use, sometimes taking Beatrix along to the studio. Millais' wife Effie had earlier been married to John Ruskin; and through this highly connected couple the Potters met even William Gladstone, just coming to the end of his long career as Britain's elder statesman. The Unitarian minister William Gaskell – husband to the famous novelist Mrs Gaskell, author of *North and South* – was another family friend. As a seventeen-year-old, hearing of Mr Gaskell's death, Beatrix would remember his kindness, and remember herself as little girl 'in a print frock and striped stockings' offering him a bunch of meadowsweet. 'Shall I really never see him again?' she lamented then, sunk in gloom, 'he is gone with almost every other, home is gone for me, the little girl does not bound about now, and live in fairyland … I have begun the dark journey of life.' But there were happier episodes – such as regular lengthy country holidays.

The Potters habitually took a house in Scotland or the north for the late summer; went away somewhere each spring so that the house in Bolton Gardens could be spring-cleaned; and visited family. Two places were particularly important in Beatrix's childhood, and one was her grandparents' home of Camfield – 'the place I love best in the world'. Everything there, she wrote later, in her twenties, was part of a perfect whole: 'the notes of the stable clock and the all-pervading smell of new-mown hay, the distant sounds of the farmyard, the feeling of plenty, well-assured, indolent wealth, honourably earned and wisely spent …'

She remembered the cuckoo calling from the oaks and the glowing autumn colours, the 'milky lemon-blue' of the snow during a white frost. The passages with their empty fire buckets, the stumpy low table where the children were allowed to make sand-pies, and the pleasure of nursery teas. 'I hope I am not by nature greedy, but there was something rapturous to us London children in the unlimited supply of new milk.' (Did the slightly rickety charms that Beatrix describes survive when the house later became Barbara Cartland's home?)

A family group taken around 1881 at Dalguise in Scotland where the Potters often holidayed, shows Beatrix at 15, her father Rupert, her young brother Bertram and her mother Helena, accompanied by their spaniel Spot.

For more than a decade, from 1871, Rupert Potter leased Dalguise on the River Tay as the family's summer residence – 'oh, it was always beautiful', wrote Beatrix nostalgically, 'home sweet home'.

The other place was Dalguise in Scotland, on the western side of the River Tay. Beatrice was barely 5 when, in 1871, her father started to lease Dalguise as the family's summer home. This to her would be a place of opportunity – of pets and pleasures shared with the father whose artistic and photographic interests she made her own. Perhaps she learnt early that the camera and the watercolour brush were just two faces of the same coin: ways to record the world around her. 'If you see anything pretty will you please send me a picture of it,' she wrote to him.

More than a decade later she would look back on Dalguise as 'home sweet home'. She remembered every stone and every tree, she said. The wind in the fir trees, the scent

Long holidays in Scotland gave Beatrix and her brother the opportunity to develop their interest in animals and insects. This page from sketchbook, labelled '1875 Dalguise', was made when Beatrix was only eight years old.

of the heather, a time when 'Everything was romantic in my imagination. The woods were peopled by the mysterious good folk … I lived in a separate world.'

In a sketchbook labelled 'Dalguise 1875' she wrote descriptions of birds' eggs and butterflies, and sketched a study of caterpillars, impressive indeed for a child just turning nine. Already she was juggling fact and fantasy – another sketch a year later shows rabbits sledging, wearing jackets and scarves. But for the moment reality won out. Extended sojurns at country houses like Dalguise allowed her to make the observations of the animal world that would stand her in such good stead.

Millais would tell Beatrix in the years ahead: 'plenty of people can *draw*, but you and my son John have observation'. And, in old age, she would tell a young relative-by-marriage: 'I believe my books have succeeded by being absolutely matter of fact, & *thorough*. The modern art student can draw, and has had training I never had in schools; but nobody seems to have the nature study & painstaking behind the actual drawing.' Here, Beatrix's apprenticeship was extraordinary.

Above Beatrix and Bertam brought two lizards back from a holiday in Ilfracombe in 1883.
Right Beatrix at 15 with Spot the spaniel, who accompanied the family everywhere by train and omnibus. He was a seasoned traveller who usually captivated the vehicle's driver.

Some of her knowledge of wildlife came from books – an interest fostered by her parents. For her tenth birthday she was enchanted to be given a copy of Mrs Blackburn's *Birds Drawn from Nature*. A decade later she was lucky enough to meet the author, and recorded in her diary Mrs Blackburn's matter-of-fact comment over the question of eating some newborn piglets who had failed to thrive on their home farm. 'I see no reason why common-sense should not foster a healthier appreciation of beauty than morbid sentimentality.'

From the start, Beatrix and Bertram's own shared interest in nature included also a degree of practical, and utterly unsentimental, experimentation; even boiling down corpses to study their skeletons. 'One of the interesting reminiscences of my early years', she recalled, 'is the memory of helping to scrape the smiling countenance of my own grandmother's deceased pig, with scalding water and the sharp-edged bottom of a brass candle-stick'.

It also included an ever-changing menagerie of pets, usual and unusual. Spot the spaniel, acquired at Dalguise, habitually travelled with the family and had to be hoisted on the railway bus in front of the luggage, setting off. 'He smiled benignly between his curls, and usually captivated the driver. He had a passion for carriage exercise. I suppose it was the dignity of the thing which pleased him … The difficulty was to prevent his riding off in omnibuses, like any other gentleman.'

March 21. 1876

March 21 1876

But the Potter children would also move around the country with a train of other, less conventional pets, like Punch the green frog, who 'had been on extensive journeys'. Beatrix would write of Toby, 'one of the lizards we brought from Ilfracombe', who had 'departed from this life in the staggers'. The menagerie also included at various times a jay and a hedgehog, rats and bats, squirrels, mice, and a whole succession of rabbits. Some credit must surely be given to the Potter parents for tolerating them all; as travelling companions when alive, and as subjects for dissection when dead.

Beatrix recorded a falcon of Bertram's, 'so tame that it is quite silly', which sat on his head and stole off his plate, and an owl – also Bertram's but less amiable – who would bite the head off a dead mouse 'and then shouts as loud as he can'. She drew the owl with a mouse's tail hanging sideways from its beak: the prototype of Old Brown in *The Tale of Squirrel Nutkin*.

'Yesterday, 19th, we bought a little ring snake fourteen inches long, it was so pretty. It hissed like fun and tied itself into knots in the road when it found it could not escape, but did not attempt to bite as the blind worms do.' The snake smelt strong but not unpleasant, whereas 'Blind worms smell like very salt shrimps gone bad.' In her powers of observation – and her powers of imagination – the foundations of Beatrix Potter's later work were being laid.

Left Though the young Beatrix made many naturalistic studies of animal life, this lively sketch of fully clad rabbits enjoying themselves on the ice, made when she was nine, already shows a strong vein of fantasy.

Alarums: 'up one day and down another'

Foundations were being laid in other senses, too. When Dalguise became unavailable for the summer holiday of 1882 it was, Beatrix said, her first great sorrow. But instead, the Potters took Wray Castle, a Victorian neo-Gothic pile in the Cumbrian Lakes. Beatrix recorded how it had been built by a doctor with his wife's money – 'Many specimen trees in the garden planted by different people. Mulberry bush planted by Wordsworth.' This, notably, was Beatrix's introduction to the Lake District she would later make her home. It was notable, too, for the fact that the vicar of Wray was one Canon Rawnsley – Hardwicke Rawnsley, a student at Oxford of John Ruskin. He would become not only a family friend but something of a mentor to Beatrix in his capacity as an amateur naturalist, as one who would very actively encourage her writing interests and as a passionate defender of the Lakeland country.

But 1882 is notable in Beatrix Potter's life for another reason also – it sees the first surviving entries in the diary she kept for the next fifteen years, in a code of her own invention, designed perhaps to shield it from her mother's prying eye. She may have begun her diary rather earlier – notes she wrote into the pages, to the effect that they are 'worth keeping', suggest that she discarded others – and it would become the record of her darker feelings. But there are brisk and decidedly unsentimental recording of the world around her, too: 'the chestnut horse is disposed of at last. Papa sent Reynolds to the Zoological Gardens to enquire the price of cat's meat: £2 for a very fat horse, 30/- for a middling one, thin ones not taken as the lions are particular.' Or 'Mr Millais is going to paint the portrait of one of the Duchess of Edinburgh's children ... Lady Mallet says the Princess of Wales has a very foreign accent.'

At the start of the next year, Beatrix was writing: 'Been to the Winter Exhibition of Old Masters at the Academy! ... I never thought there *could* be such pictures. It is almost too much to see them all at once – just fancy seeing five magnificent Van Dyck's side by side, before me who never thought to see one. It is rather a painful pleasure, but I have seldom felt such a great one.' The question of her own artistic training was becoming a major theme.

When Dalguise ceased to be available for their holidays the Potters instead took the neo-Gothic Wray Castle, on the western side of Windermere. It is now run by the National Trust.

Beatrix's sojurn on Windermere. the largest of the Lakes, marked the start of her long relationship with the area, and particularly with this southern region of the Lake District which would be her chosen home. Trips on the Windermere ferry (seen in the background) remained a feature of her life.

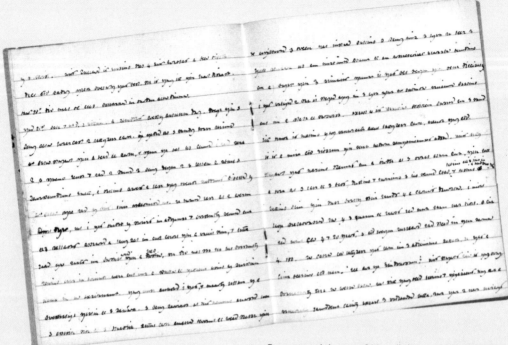

From around the age of 14 until she was 30, Beatrix Potter kept a diary written in a code of her own invention, possibly to shield it from her mother's eyes.

Beatrix was now in her seventeenth year and, as she wrote on April 25th, 'one day up and down another. Have been a long way down today, and now my head feels empty and I am nothing in particular. Will things never settle? Is this being grown-up?' Her mother's arbitrary employment of a new governess, a Miss Carter, had just seemed to signal an end to her hopes, 'cutting off more and more time for painting … Only a year, but if it is like the last it will be a lifetime – I can't settle to any thing but my painting. I lost my patience over everything else.' But Annie Carter, only three years older than her charge, would play an important role in Beatrix's later life.

For five years she had been having drawing lessons with a Miss Cameron: 'I have great reason to be grateful to her, though we were not on particularly good terms for the last good while. I have learnt from her freehand, model, geometry, perspective, and a little water-colour flower painting.' But if you and your master are determined to look at nature and art in two different directions, she wrote, 'you are sure to stick'.

Going now to study with a 'Mrs A' , she had similar reservations, convinced that though technique could be taught, art 'lies chiefly with oneself'. After going to Mrs A for the second time, 'is the money being thrown away, will it even do me harm? … I think and hope my self-will which brings me into so many scrapes will guard me here – but it is tiresome, when you do get some lessons, to be taught in a way you dislike and to have to swallow your feelings out of consideration at home and there.'

Home life was becoming more difficult – Bertram by now was away at school, 'leaving me the responsibility of a precious bat. It is a charming little creature, quite tame and apparently happy as long as it has sufficient flies and raw meat.' Bertram's departure left Beatrix even more lonely. It's hard not to see significance in way that in 1884, the handwriting in which she wrote her coded diary grew dramatically smaller. There was still much comment on public events: 'I really wish I had more time and I would keep an historical account … Latest news, attempt to blow up Salisbury cathedral.' But she was not, as she wrote in January 1884, in high spirits. That summer: 'I am eighteen today … I feel as if I had been going on such a time.'

Benjamin Bunny, known as Bounce, was one of a series of pet rabbits Beatrix owned – a 'charming rascal', she called him, 'amiably sentimental to the verge of silliness, at the next . . . a demon, throwing himself on his back, scratching and spluttering.'

Another pet which Beatrix would draw was her dormouse Xarifa, a character in *The Fairy Caravan* (1929) – 'a most sweet person, but slumbrous'. This 1885 photograph shows Beatrix with her hair cropped after a recent illness.

Art was a refuge for Beatrix. 'It is all the same, drawing, painting, modelling, the irresistible urge to copy any beautiful object which strikes the eye. Why cannot one be content to look at it? I cannot rest, I must draw, however poor the result, and when I have a bad time come over me it is a stronger desire than ever, and settles on the queerest things … Last time, in the middle of September, I caught myself in the back yard making a careful and admiring copy of the swill bucket, and the laugh it gave me brought me round.' After experimenting with a number of forms, from oil painting to etching, the watercolour was emerging as her natural form, and through the years ahead the watercolours she made of well-loved places – images which might or might not make their way indirectly into her books – would bear witness to her talent.

In the winter, coming back to London from Camfield: 'I do wish we lived in the country. I have been perfectly well in mind and body these few days … I wish for many things, and yet how much I have to be thankful for, but these odious fits of low spirits would spoil any life.' Christmas was not necessarily celebrated by Unitarians, but Beatrice was in no mood for even a limited acknowledgement: 'Xmas comes but once a year – thank goodness … General depression. I wonder how they all feel underground?'

She was ill the following spring and the end of March saw 'a lamentable falling off'. In what was then a standard treatment for a fever, she 'had my few remaining locks clipped short at Douglas's. Draughty. My hair nearly all came off since I was ill. Now that the sheep is shorn, I may say without pride that I have seldom seen a more beautiful head of hair than mine. Last summer it was very thick and within about four inches of my knees, being more than a yard long.'

Weeks later she was managing to joke about her loss. 'I always thought I was born to be a discredit to my parents, but it was exhibited in a marked manner today.' Her hat blew off her shorn head and into a fountain by the Kensington exhibition. 'If only I had not been with papa, he does not often take me out, and I doubt he will do it again for a time.' She was still feeling the effects of her illness. 'How is it these high-heeled ladies who dine out, paint and pinch their waists to deformity, can racket about all day long, while I who sleep o'nights, can turn in my stays, and dislike sweets and dinners, am so tired towards the end of the afternoon that I can scarcely keep my feet? It is very hard and strange, I wonder if it will always be so.' In later years Beatrix would observe how, once free to live the life she chose in the country, her health would improve dramatically.

But she was now, as she grew, leading a fuller life in London – going to exhibitions, to the theatre, to the new Natural History Museum. She had even an approximation of a coming out, when her parents gave a party for her, shortly before she turned 19. Her first party for ten years, she noted, 'and for my part may it suffice for ten more'; but all the same 'I enjoyed myself, and, contrary to my own and parents' expectations, behaved well.' But there seems to have been no follow up, no likelihood of marriage taking Beatrix on to the next stage of a nineteenth-century woman's life.

Hearing the news that a cousin had made an imprudent marriage: 'Love in a cottage is sentimental, but the parties must be very pleasing to each other to make it tolerable ... If this is what beauty leads to, I am well content to have a red nose and a shorn head,' she decided. 'I may be lonely, but better that than an unhappy marriage.' Childhood still clung about her, and though she noted the day, '9th July', on which her education formally finished (Annie Carter was wedding a civil engineer called Edwin Moore), that fact may simply have reminded her that she had nothing else to do.

On New Year's Eve 1885, she looked back gloomily: 'Much bitterness and a few peaceful summer days ... I wonder why one is so unwilling to let go this old year? not because it has been joyful, but because I fear its successors – I am terribly afraid of the future.' The following year her code writing was so cramped and tiny she could cram more than 1500 words onto one small page. She was 'myself middling, past being low, reached the stage of indifference and morbid curiosity'.

In the winter of 1886/7 she was ill again, catching up with her diary only months later: 'I am writing this at the end of June, having been very ill with something uncommonly like rheumatic fever ... Very little fever, great deal of rheumatics. Could not be turned in bed without screaming out ... We were in a deplorable state all round.' Bertram too had been ill; her mother 'at her wits end'; her father concerned about family affairs.

Benjamin was the model for the first drawings Beatrix sold, in 1890, a set of six Christmas cards for the publisher Hildesheimer and Faulkner. On hearing the good news 'My first act was to give Bounce (what an investment that rabbit has been in spite of the hutches), a cupful of hemp seeds . . . Next morning he was partially intoxicated and wholly unmanageable.'

But ordinary life went on – or ordinary for the Potters, anyway: Beatrix's packing list for the family's spring trip of March 1889 is an instructive one. Amid notes to self 'To see about old dresses', 'Dentist', and 'Knitting' comes '2 bird's skeletons', and 'Paint stoat's eyes'. But, perhaps significantly, it seems as if there was very little diary writing for the next few years. Beatrix was experimenting with other, real-life, opportunities.

Even within the family circle, she did have allies. Her brother Bertram was growing up – not always easily, already displaying signs of the vulnerability that would lead him to alcoholism in later years. But his vulnerability may have made him all the more sympathetic to Beatrix's difficulties. And one important ally was Rupert Potter's brother-in-law, the chemist and Member of Parliament Sir Henry Enfield Roscoe. When for Christmas 1889 Beatrix painted place cards and Christmas cards for the family, it was her uncle Roscoe who suggested that her work was worthy of a wider audience. Both Beatrix and her brother were eager to find a way of getting a little money of their own – and thus a little independence.

The following May Beatrix was writing about how she and Bertram had decided 'that I should make a grand effort in the way of Christmas Cards … So in the beginning of February I began privately to prepare Six Designs, taking for my Model that charming rascal Benjamin Bouncer our tame Jack Hare … I was rather impeded by the inquisitiveness of my aunt, and the idiosyncrasies of Benjamin who has an appetite for certain sorts of paint, but the cards were finished by Easter.' The first publisher sent them back by return of post: but the second made an offer.

'My first act was to give Bounce (what an investment that rabbit has been in spite of the hutches), a cupful of hemp seeds, the consequence being that when I wanted to draw him next morning he was partially intoxicated and wholly unmanageable. Then I retired to bed, and lay awake chuckling till 2 in the morning, and afterwards had an impression that Bunny came to my bedside in a white cotton night cap and tickled me with his whiskers.'

At the age of 24 she could see her designs published, first as Christmas and New Year cards, and then as illustration to a seven-page booklet of verses by one Frederic E. Weatherly, *The Happy Pair*. Beatrix sent some sketches to the publisher Frederick Warne & Co, suggesting a further booklet: they wrote back saying they were not in the market for small productions of that sort, but that 'if at any time you have any ideas & drawings in book form: we should be happy to give them our consideration'. The idea did not bear fruit for a long time – but a seed had been sown.

Adventures: 'a good summer's work'

It seems significant, looking back, that it was in 1892 – from the family's annual spring trip, which this year had taken them to Falmouth – that Beatrix Potter wrote the first of the picture letters that would eventually give birth to her books. Her one-time governess Annie Chapman had married, and Beatrix was fond of visiting Annie Moore and her growing family. Her diary, too shows her trying out writing in various forms, experimenting with descriptions of people and place.

The family spent that summer in Scotland, at Birnam near Dalguise. 'Benjamin Bunny travelled in a covered basket in the wash-place; took him out of the basket near Dunbar, but proved scared and bit the family.' Benjamin Bunny, known as Bounce, would be the chief of Beatrix's pet rabbits to inspire her most famous creation; and photographs of her taking Benjamin out on a lead are surely as fantastical as anything in the *Peter Rabbit* story.

'After breakfast taking Mr. Benjamin Bunny to pasture at the edge of the cabbage bed with his leather dog-lead, I heard a rustling' she recorded in her journal, 'and out came a little wild rabbit to talk to him, it crept half across the cabbage bed and then sat up on its hind legs, apparently grunting. I replied, but the stupid Benjamin did nothing but stuff cabbage. The little animal evidently a female, and of a shabby appearance, nibbling, advanced … face twitching with excitement and admiration for the beautiful Benjamin …'

A couple of weeks later: 'Benjamin's mind has at last comprehended gooseberries, he stands up and picks them off the bush, but has such a comical little mouth, it is a sort of bob cherry business.' Alas, his mouth was also managing to encompass a number of peppermints fed to him by the gamekeeper and tooth problems would eventually bring a premature end to his life.

When Benjamin accompanied Beatrix away on holiday she used to take
him out on a leather dog lead to graze on the cabbages in the vegetable
garden – much to the amusement of the servants.

"That is Not a
fat pigeon

This illustration for Aesop's fable 'The Fox and the Grapes' recalls a real tamed fox Beatrix had
known, 'so sly, it had a habit of saving a portion of porridge within reach of his chain, then
pretending sleep and pouncing on the hens, which it took into the kennel "feathers and all"'.

'Rabbits', Beatrix wrote, 'are creatures of warm volatile temperament but shallow and absurdly transparent'. Her many diary entries about the species that would make her famous were not confined to her pets. Freeing a rabbit from a snare that autumn: 'I warmed it at the fire, relieved it from a number of fleas, and it came round … They are regular vermin, but one cannot stand by to see a thing mauled about from one's friendship for the race.'

Beatrix was observing animal behaviour in the wild as well as enjoying the idiosyncrasies of those she knew best. A heron swallowing four fish in quick succession, the first digested while the last was still in its mouth; the way partridges will make their nests even on railway tracks; the habits of the deer and the differences between breeds of cattle. Following in her father's footsteps she was now a keen amateur photographer, and this too fostered her powers of observation. Going to photograph a tame fox she recorded how the Scottish gamekeeper had trapped one in a snare, and was amused to notice it played dead until he had carried it home. 'It lived for six years in a kennel and fed upon porridge. It was so sly, it had a habit of saving a portion of porridge within reach of his chain, then pretending sleep and pouncing on the hens, which it took into the kennel "feathers and all".' She drew a fox with a chain round its neck, and it's hard to doubt that his cunning gave birth to her later creation, Mr Tod. Ever alive to an animal's personality, Beatrix loved tales of their unexpected or fantastical behaviour – like the local story of a pony who swam across a loch to get home.

But Beatrix was extending her observation of the natural world beyond the curious or the quaint, and into the realm of the scientific. This was perhaps the last great heyday of the amateur scientist – and of the generalist, who would soon be supplanted by the professional specialists – and since Bertram went away to school Beatrix had been making good use of his old microscope, and drawing what she saw. But she had also for several years begun painting fungi, and this was the field on which she was to concentrate. Of all hopeless things to draw, 'I should think the very worst is a fine fat fungus', she wrote in October – but before the family left Birnam she was able to show her drawings to a fellow amateur of mycology.

Eastwood Dunkeld
Sep 4th 93

My dear Noel,
          I don't know what to
write to you, so I shall tell you a story
          about four little rabbits.
                    whose names were—

Flopsy, Mopsy   Cottontail

                              and Peter

They lived with their mother in a
sand bank under the root of a
big fir tree.

Left The picture letter Beatrix Potter wrote to Noel Moore, the son of her old governess, on 4 September 1893 saw the birth of one of the most famous characters in literature – Peter Rabbit. As so often, he was based on a real pet – Beatrix's new rabbit Peter Piper.
Above 'My rabbit Peter is so lazy, he lies before the fire in a box, with a little rug,' Beatrix wrote.

Charlie McIntosh – 'that learned but extremely shy man' – was the postman at Dalguise. An Inver native, he had worked at the local sawmill before losing all the fingers of one hand in an accident. More to the point, observation on his rural round had made him a notable amateur naturalist. Very tall and thin, with watering eyes and nose he was, Beatrix said, a 'startled scarecrow' of a man. 'I would not make fun of him for worlds, but he reminded me so much of a damaged lamp post.' But he was also, she insisted, 'a perfect dragon of erudition', persuaded to come out of his shell by the sight of the drawings Beatrix had made, at which 'his mouth evidently watered'.

He promised to send her samples of fungi to record, and when Beatrix had returned to Bolton Gardens, they began to correspond with formality and humour – 'Miss Potter trusts Mr McIntosh will never send a horrid plant like a white stick with a loose cap, which smells exactly like a dead sheep! She went to look at a fine specimen but could not find the courage to draw it.' Their collaboration must have given an extra boost to the enthusiasm Beatrice would have felt for the family's spending next summer again by the banks of the Tay.

This time she took with her a new rabbit, Peter Piper, 'bought at a very tender age, in the Uxbridge Road, Shepherd's Bush, for the exorbitant sum of 4/6'. Like his predecessor, Benjamin, he would learn to do tricks. ('Peter Rabbit was the

entertainment', she wrote a year later, but 'it is tiresome that he never will show off. He really is good at tricks when hungry, in private, jumping … ringing little bell and drumming on a tambourine.') From Dunkeld this year, on September 4 1893, she wrote not the first but easily the most famous picture letter to Noel Moore, Annie's eldest child, whom illness forced to spend much time in bed.

'My dear Noel,
I don't know what to write to you, so I shall tell you a story about four little rabbits whose names were Flopsy, Mopsy, Cottontail and Peter. They lived with their mother in a sand bank under the roof of a big fir tree.
"Now, my dears", said old Mrs Bunny, "you may go into the field or down the lane, but don't go into Mr McGregor's garden."'

Beatrix always denied she had known any gardener called McGregor, but the McGregor of the letter looks just like her description of Charlie McIntosh the year before. The very day before she wrote to Noel, she had been able to send to McIntosh a drawing of the extremely localised pine cone fungus she had found – *Strobilomyces strobilaceus*, the 'old man of the woods'. The day after, she wrote another letter, to Noel's younger brother Eric.

'Once upon a time there was a frog called Mr Jeremy Fisher and he lived in a little house on the bank of a river.' This Jeremy went fishing for a minnow but found he'd caught instead a spiney stickleback and wound up eating 'roasted grass-hopper with lady-bird sauce'. But the genesis of Beatrix Potter's (and Jeremy Fisher's) later *Tale* would be also the fishponds at Melford Hall in Suffolk, where her cousin had in 1890 married the baronet, William Hyde Parker, and where Beatrix often stayed; and the 'greedy pike' she had noticed among the waterlilies while staying at Keswick some eight years before.

The next year, 1894, from Falmouth Beatrix would again write to Noel with what many years later would prove to be the genesis of her last 'Little Book' – about having seen a pig with a curly tail aboard a ship, the *Pearl of Falmouth*. 'I dare say it enjoys the

Left Beatrix often stayed at Melford Hall in Suffolk, home of her cousin Ethel, and loved the views across the ponds towards the sixteenth-century manor house. She would try out stories on the children there.

sail but when the sailors get hungry they eat it. If that pig had any sense it would slip down into the boat at the end of the ship and row away.' That, almost four decades later, would be exactly what Little Pig Robinson does. She drew in the letter a fantasy of the pig 'living on Robinson Crusoe's Island, where it lived for years and grew 'very very fat' – just, again, like the hero of her book.

That June, Beatrix made another visit, to relatives at Harescombe in Gloucestershire, this time travelling without her family … 'so much of an event in the eyes of my relations that they made it appear an undertaking to me'. She had not been away 'independently' for five years. This visit too was perhaps important – Beatrix wrote at length about her cousin Caroline Hutton, who urged the visit on her, and about Caroline's independence. Beatrix may not have agreed with all Caroline's modern theories – 'Latter day fate ordains that many women shall be unmarried and self-contained, nor should I personally dream to complain, but I hold an old-fashioned notion that a happy marriage is the crown of a woman's life.' All the same, Caroline's words may have fallen on receptive ground.

Days before, Beatrix had written to the German firm of art printers Ernest Nister: 'I have received your letter of 2nd inst with reference to the pen & ink drawings, but regret to inform you that I am not satisfied with your terms …' From the start she knew how to place a proper value on her work. But it is also notable that she was becoming more open about the dissatisfaction she felt all around.

That summer's holiday to Lennel, on the Scottish borders brought many enjoyable finds. Beatrix had also become an amateur of paleontology, perhaps encouraged by the Hutton family's serious interest in fossils, and was lucky enough quickly to come across some fossilized fish teeth – and later, as the fungi season began, 'an ideal heavenly dream of the toadstool eaters' in the woods near Hatchednize. 'The fungus starred the ground apparently in thousands, a dozen sorts in sight at once … *Cortinarius* and the handsome *Lactarius deliciosus* being conspicuous, and joy of joys, the spiky *Gomphidius glutinosus*, a round, slimy, purple head among the moss'. But she was finding it difficult to juggle her expeditions with her mother's demands on the carriage, and found it 'exasperating' to have to leave the area, with her family, just as the fungi 'begin to come in crowds'.

On what would prove to be their last Scottish holiday, her movements were still not her own. 'I was very sorry indeed to come away, with a feeling of not having half worked through the district, but I have done a good summer's work. The funguses will come up again and the fossils will keep. I hope I may go back again some day when I am an old woman, unless I happen to become a fossil myself, which would save trouble.'

In the same journal entry, she wrote about fungi in terms which show her interest moving in a new, more scientific, direction. ' I see no mystery in the enlarging ring myself. The funguses grow from the mycelium, not the spore direct, and the mycelium grows from that spore which falls outwards on unexhausted ground.' There had long been uncertainty about exactly how fungi – those strange entities, owing as much to the animal as to the plant kingdom – reproduced themselves; but it was a mystery Beatrix began to feel she might solve.

Among a number of souvenirs Beatrix left at Melford Hall is this ink drawing in the visitors' book, made on a visit of 1912.

Experiments: 'a fine fat fungus'

In the autumn and winter of 1895, Beatrix was working on twelve entomological illustrations for Morley Memorial College, a working-man's educational establishment based in what is now the Old Vic theatre, whose Unitarian principal was an old family acquaintance. Her research took her to the Natural History Museum but she found it frustratingly awkward to get any information from the gentleman clerks: 'If people are forward I can manage them, but if they take the line of being shocked it is perfectly awful to a shy person.'

She had, again through her family's Unitarian connections, been introduced to the Museum's director, Sir William Flower, but was distressed when he twice failed to recognize her. 'Must confess to crying after I got home, my father being as usual deplorable.' (A year later: 'I wonder why I never seem to know people,' she mused. 'It makes one wonder whether one is presentable. It strikes me it is the way to make one not.') All the same, the Morley commission was a way ahead: this was once again paid work. In December 1895 she was writing of 'the comfort of having money. One must make out some way. It is something to have a little money to spend on books and to look forward to being independent, though forlorn.'

But Beatrix was beginning to think of moving beyond the stage of drawings – from observation to experimentation, and to theory; and the spring of 1896 gave her opportunity. Her uncle Sir Henry Roscoe (that year appointed vice-chancellor of the University of London) promised to get her a ticket to the Royal Botanic Gardens at Kew; not then a garden open to the public but only to scientists working on a specific project (and a place where the three female workers were told to wear a costume guaranteed not to inflame their male colleagues' desire).

Right The many paintings Beatrix made of fungi are sufficiently detailed and accurate still to be used as study aids today. This example of the conical brittlestem fungus (*Psathyrella conopilus*) was found at Ford in Northumberland on 11 August 1894.

This watercolour of Esthwaite Water is one of many expressing Beatrix's love for the Lake District. 'I have often been laughed at for thinking Esthwaite Water the most beautiful of the Lakes.'

Her first visit to Kew took place on May 19, when Sir Henry impulsively took her to meet the gardens' director, Mr Thistleton-Dyer, and 'I only hope I shall remember separately the five different gentlemen with whom I had the honour of shaking hands.' The Director 'seemed pleased with my drawings and a little surprised' – a mixture of cautious welcome and condescension which was to prove typical of her reception by the scientific establishment. Trailing behind the men as they talked to each other she had, she wrote, the 'amusing feeling of being regarded as young'. In June she returned, to see the man whose interests most jumped with hers, George Massee who 'has passed several stages of development into a fungus himself – I am occasionally conscious of a similar transformation'. That summer in the Lakes she was successfully germinating spores – and formulating the idea that fungi have an underground form, a mould, and it is this that enables them to spread.

It clearly suited her to have a purpose. On 28 July, 'I am thirty this day', she wrote. 'I feel much younger at thirty than I did at twenty; firmer and stronger both in mind and body. Coincidentally or otherwise this was the first summer holiday that had brought her to stay at Lakefield (now Ees Wyke) on Esthwaite Water. Brought her, in other words, to the village of Near Sawrey which would later become her home: 'such a pretty place', she wrote in a picture letter to Noel, 'and we have a boat on Esthwaite Lake'. She described to him the rushes and the beds of water lilies, the wild ducks and the lapwing, and the farmer's 'beautiful fat pig'.

'I prefer a pastoral landscape backed by mountains.' People laughed at her for thinking Esthwaite Water the most beautiful of the Lakes, she said once, but: 'It really strikes me that some scenery is almost theatrical, or ultra-romantic.' When autumn came she would be: 'very sorry to come away in spite of the broken weather. It is as nearly perfect a little place as I ever lived in, and such nice old-fashioned people in the village.'

'I think one of my pleasantest memories of Esthwaite is sitting on Oatmeal Crag on a Sunday afternoon, where there is a sort of table of rock with a dip, with the lane and fields and oak copse like in a trough below my feet, and all the little tiny fungus people singing and bobbing and dancing in the grass and under the leaves … What heaven can be more real than to retain the spirit-world of childhood, tempered and balanced by knowledge and common-sense, to fear no longer the terror that flieth by night, yet to feel truly and understand a little, a very little, of the story of life.' This was clearly her future – but there was still the unfinished business of the fungi to conclude.

On her return to Bolton Gardens, Beatrix 'escaped out of the house quite early' and went to share with her uncle her theories, and the fact that she had succeeded in germinating spores. He invented 'a fishing letter' to George Massee at Kew, trying to find out whether anyone else was working along the same lines. But it was soon evident that Massee himself 'knew very little about it'.

Beatrix herself was working in far from ideal conditions – trying to produce laboratory-standard evidence in the household kitchens – but nonetheless, she was doing something new. She purchased a more powerful magnifying lens, she took practical advice from former associates of her uncle's – and, on December 3, she went back to see Thistleton-Dyer, explaining (perhaps rather tactlessly) that her uncle was satisfied with her work, and felt Kew's director should look at it.

Perhaps it was some consciousness of awkwardness that explains what came next. Waiting in Thistleton-Dyer's office, Beatrix was overcome by shyness and 'incontinently fled'. (Her confidence had not been helped by the fact that her father insisted on going though her work.) But she had a new theory, now, about hybridisation and the role that lichens (half fungus, half algae) could play, and under its impetus she went back a few days later and 'had it up and down' with the director.

He was dismissive of her theories: Massee, to his credit, was not, while her uncle's reaction to what he perceived as a snub to his own prestige was to suggest – if she were *quite* sure' – that her work should be presented in a paper for the prestigious Linnean Society of London. Beatrix describes herself as being 'convulsed with amusement' at the fuss, but as the new year dawned she was surely nervous, though convinced of her correctness, ('Upon the subject of chlorophyll and symbiosis I am afraid I am unpleasant …').

On January 12 she wrote to Charlie McIntosh: ' Have you ever suspected that there are *intermediate* species amongst *Agarics* and *Boleti*? We [Beatrix and her uncle] are strongly of the opinion for certain good reasons that there are mixed fungi – that is to say – either growing actually upon a mixed network of *mycelium*, or else hybrid species which have originated in that way.' In pursuance of her research she had bribed a workman to give her some samples of dry rot, but had had to hide the paper bag in the garden. Even her parents' devotion to science might not be enough to make them welcome it to the house.

Unfortunately it is at this moment that Beatrix's journal ends, and with it the direct record of her feelings. On 31 January 1897, her last entry, she was in a state of 'disgraceful and abject fright' at the thought of taking her research to the Professor of Botany at Cambridge, as had been recommended, and convinced that Thistleton-Dyer was 'something of a misogynist … but it is odious to a shy person to be snubbed as conceited, especially when the shy person happened to be right'.

But on 1 April (April Fool's Day!) the Proceedings of the Linnean Society record a paper being read, 'On the Germination of the Spores of the *Agaricineae*' by Miss Helen B. Potter. The paper was sponsored by George Massee since, as a woman, Beatrix could not do it herself. The paper was 'laid upon the table', ie put out for members' consideration. Although Massee said it was well received the Linnean, however, decided not to publish it. That, at least, is one conclusion to be drawn from the fact that the Society's records, a week later, show Miss Potter as having withdrawn it. Either they or she had decided more work was necessary.

The original paper has long been lost – but perhaps in getting it so far Beatrix, as an outsider to the scientific establishment, and a woman to boot, had already done something extraordinary. All the more so, of course, for the fact that her theories about the reproduction of fungi – a complex problem which would take years to solve – are accepted today.

Beatrix may have gone on with her research for a time, but she must have decided that mycology – and the world of the professional scientist – was not where her future lay. That summer was spent at Lingholm, near Keswick in the northern Lakes, and in August Beatrix was writing of an altogether lighter subject: 'There is a lady who lives on an island on the lake who told me some curious things about animals swimming . . . Also when her nuts are ripe, squirrels appear on the island, but she has not seen them coming. There is an American story that squirrels go down the rivers on little rafts, using their tails for sails, but I think the Keswick squirrels must swim.' For *The Tale of Squirrel Nutkin*, of course, Beatrix would prefer the raft theory.

The Potters would stay at Lingholm also in subsequent years, meeting there Hardwicke Rawnsley who had moved from Wray to the edge of Keswick. Generally, however, Rupert Potter's failing health meant that they were travelling less. In some ways, perhaps, horizons were closing in for Beatrice. But perversely, maybe that is what was needed to force her to find her own way ahead. The single most important visit she made in these years was in January 1900, to Annie Moore – who suggested that the picture letters Beatrix had written to the Moore children might possibly have the makings of a little book.

A new idea for a new century: and what an idea it would prove to be.

Peter Rabbit

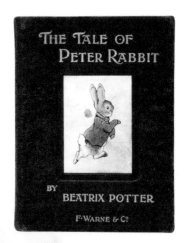

Beatrix disliked 'that idiotic prancing rabbit' on the cover of Frederick Warne's edition. But *The Tale of Peter Rabbit* (1901/2) was the book that made her name.

T he rebellious little rabbit in his blue coat has become one of the most iconic figures in children's literature – the brand name often used to comprise all of Beatrix Potter's work. But the preference rather annoyed Peter Rabbit's creator: 'at one time I almost loathed *Peter Rabbit*, I was so sick of him,' Beatrix wrote.

But this, of course, was the book that made her name – a runaway bestseller from the time Frederick Warne first published it in 1902. Even then, it had had a long and complicated history – a picture letter to the son of Beatrix's old governess; a verse chronicle never published; an edition privately printed for Beatrix herself. Indeed, you might say that the genesis goes even further back – Beatrix was only ten or eleven when, in 1877, William Gaskell sent his 'kind regards' to a pet rabbit of Beatrix's called Tommy.

But it was a subsequent pet, Benjamin Bouncer or 'Bounce', who Beatrix described as the inspiration for her character. '"Peter" was drawn from a very intelligent Belgian hare called Bounce', she wrote later in life (the Belgian 'hare' is actually a kind of rabbit). 'A noisy cheerful determined animal, inclined to attack strangers.' She described on many occasions Bounce's habit of growling at strange workmen, how one moment the vulgar Mr. Benjamin Bunny could be 'amiably sentimental to the verge of silliness, at the next … a demon, throwing himself on his back, scratching and spluttering'. No-one who has seen pictures of Benjamin on a dog lead would doubt that, as Beatrix once wrote in a letter to *The Field*, 'even the usually idiotic hutch rabbit is capable of developing strong character, if taken in hand when quite young'.

Benjamin was succeeded by another rabbit – called Peter, or Peter Piper. In February 1895 Beatrix sent a picture letter to Noel Moore: 'My rabbit Peter is so lazy, he lies before the fire in a box, with a little rug. His claws grew too long, quite

uncomfortable, so I tried to cut them with scissors
… ' But his gentle temperament sounds far less
like the character in Beatrix's book. After this 'Peter
Rabbit' died, aged 9, in January 1901, Beatrix wrote
his disposition was 'uniformly amiable and his temper
unfailingly sweet'.

Peter squeezes under Mr McGregor's
gate to stuff himself with lettuces, French
beans and radishes before having to flee.

The Peter of the book is 'very naughty'. Warned by his
mother not to go into Mr McGregor's garden – 'Your father
had an accident there; he was put into a pie' – he sets off
immediately. Squeezing under the garden gate, scoffing
lettuces and broad beans, radishes and parsley, only to be spotted by Mr McGregor, he escapes
with the greatest difficulty. His story, across the world, has sold more than 40 million copies.

'Peter never aspired to be high art – he was passable … but if not high art his moderate price
has at least enabled him to reach many hundreds of thousands of children, and has given
them pleasure without ugliness' wrote Beatrix modestly.

Timeline
1893 Beatrix sends a picture letter to Noel Moore: 'My dear Noel, I don't know what to write
to you, so I shall tell you a story about four little rabbits whose names were Flopsy, Mopsy
Cottontail and Peter … '

1900 Beatrix decides to turn the picture letter into a book, but initially meets with no success.

1901 Beatrix arranges to have the book privately printed, while her friend Hardwicke
Rawnsley, himself the published author of children's poetry, puts the story into verse. The
privately printed version is ready in December and, Beatrix writes, 'going off very well
amongst my friends and relations'. Meanwhile, the publishers Frederick Warne & Co agree to
bring out a version for the book trade, using Beatrix's own words rather than Rawnsley's verse
(see page 65).

1902 A shortened version of the book is published in October by Frederick Warne – who by
the end of the year have printed 28,000 copies to cope with demand. It goes to a sixth printing
within a year – 'what an appalling quantity of Peter,' Beatrix says.

1903 Pirated editions of *Peter Rabbit* begin to appear in America, where the copyright had not been registered. At the end of the year Beatrix herself makes the first Peter Rabbit doll, and registers the patent.

1904 In Beatrix's follow-up *The Tale of Benjamin Bunny*, Peter and his cousin Benjamin retrieve his clothes from Mr McGregor's garden, but have to be rescued from a cat.

1909 Now an adult, and helping his mother run a nursery garden, Peter plays a small role in *The Tale of the Flopsy Bunnies* (about the children of his cousin Benjamin and sister Flopsy). The same year he can also be glimpsed in *The Tale of Ginger and Pickles*.

1911 *Peter Rabbit's Painting Book* is published.

1912 In *The Tale of Mr Tod*, Peter helps his cousin rescue his children from kidnap by the badger Tommy Brock.

1917 Warne ask Beatrix to allow them to protest about an illustrated booklet by Ernest A. Aris featuring a rabbit called Peter.

9p

The Tale of Peter Rabbit
The Year of the Child

Left From the start, Beatrix was much concerned with the merchandising of Peter Rabbit. She herself made the first Peter toy, but she continued to be troubled by cheap unauthorised copies.
Middle The Year of the Child in 1979 saw the issue of a Peter Rabbit stamp.
Right Oscar-winning actress Emma Thompson was already a longstanding Potter fan when she was asked to continue Beatrix's work by writing further Peter Rabbit stories.

1920 Plagiarism would continue to be a problem, especially in America. *The decade sees endless unauthorised sequels, including in 1927 Peter Rabbit's Wedding.*

1924 Beatrix first assists the Invalid Children's Aid Association to raise money for a Peter Rabbit hospital bed. Over the next years she produces Christmas cards featuring a variety of animals to help the Peter Rabbit Fund raise money for four more beds.

1928 *Peter Rabbit's Almanac* (for 1929).

1935 Beatrix is visited by Christopher Le Fleming, who has composed piano pieces inspired by Peter Rabbit.

1936 Walt Disney writes to Beatrix asking for permission to make a film of Peter Rabbit, but Beatrix fears her drawings are not good enough to be enlarged for the big screen.

1979 In the Year of the Child, the UK Post Office issues a *Tale of Peter Rabbit* stamp.

1992–5 *The World of Peter Rabbit and his friends*, 6 half hour animated films.

2002 Warne publish a centenary edition, adding six illustrations deleted from the 1903 version.

2003 Formation of the Friends of Peter Rabbit Club.

2012 CGI-animated *Peter Rabbit* series, featuring a new female character, Lily Bobtail. Frederick Warne publish *The Further Tale of Peter Rabbit* by actress Emma Thompson – a tribute to Beatrix's Scottish visits. Thompson subsequently writes two other Peter Rabbit stories.

2013 Peter Rabbit is pictured in unlikely company when press seize on the story that Prince George's nursery has been decorated with a Beatrix Potter theme. The Middleton family are distantly related to Beatrix Potter.

2016 Peter Rabbit appears on a coin issued by the Royal Mint to mark the 150th anniversary of his creator's birth, while an older Peter makes a guest appearance in the posthumously published *Tale of Kitty-in-Boots*.

Part II

1900–1913

Acceptance: 'these little books'

A portrait of Beatrix Potter taken 1905–10, at around the age of 40.,

As she set out on the road towards publication Beatrix's first step, in the spring of 1900, had been to ask the Moore children whether they still had her letters. Luckily, they had cherished them. Beatrix set to work expanding the story of Peter Rabbit she had sent to Noel, adding in more about Peter's attempts to escape from Mr McGregor's garden. She sent it off – in a lined exercise book, with black-and-white illustrations, and a colour frontispiece – but it came back from publisher after publisher, though one was sufficiently interested to suggest a larger format book, which Beatrix refused.

Early in March she wrote to Marjorie Moore: 'You will begin to be afraid I have run away with the letters altogether! I will keep them a little longer because I want to make a list of them, but I don't think they will be made into a book this time because the publisher wants poetry. The publisher is a gentleman who prints books, and he wants a bigger book than he has got enough money to pay for! and Miss Potter has arguments with him … I think Miss Potter will go off to another publisher soon! She would rather make 2 or 3 little books costing 1/ each than one big book costing 6/ because she thinks little rabbits cannot afford to spend 6 shillings for one book and would never buy it.' The pictures on the letter show a long skirted figure, Beatrix herself, confronting a gentleman in a frock coat – and two little rabbits making their choice from bookshelves, while their mother rummages in her purse.

The idea that the story might be saleable in verse must have originated with Hardwicke Rawnsley, whom Beatrix had consulted and who had himself published children's poetry. Helpfully, he set about versifying Beatrix's story:

Beatrix Potter with Canon Hardwicke Rawnsley, a founder of the
National Trust and an important influence in her life.

Norman Warne with one of his nephews. Norman was one of three brothers
who ran F. Warne & Co, her publisher.

There were four little bunnies
no bunnies were sweeter
Mopsy and Cotton-tail
Flopsy and Peter

Meanwhile, Beatrix had decided to publish the story herself, just as she wanted it, with a quantity of black-and-white illustrations. She consulted a friend about finding a printer – Gertrude Woodward of the Natural History Museum, whose sister also illustrated children's books. On Gertrude's advice, she ordered 250 copies from Strangeways & Sons.

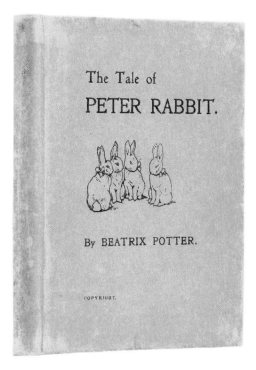

The privately printed edition of *Peter Rabbit* had far more illustrations than the Frederick Warne one, but almost entirely in black and white.

Both the coloured illustration of Peter Rabbit being put to bed and the black and white drawing of the whole rabbit family come from the Frederick Warne edition of the book.

Beatrix made extensive use of the buildings around the cathedral for *The Tailor of Gloucester* (left), her own favourite among the 'little books'. One (right) is now a shop and museum devoted to her life and work.

Events, however, had been moving on. Rawnsley's poetical version of *Peter Rabbit* had been sent out anew to publishers – and the company of Frederick Warne reacted with qualified enthusiasm. They preferred a 'simple narration' to Rawnsley's moralistic verse, they wanted fewer illustrations and all of them in colour, but if that could be arranged, then …

On December 18, 1901 Beatrix wrote to F. Warne & Co to thrash out the practicalities (and explain that she was already committed to the first, the private edition); a letter very businesslike as to royalties and copyright: 'I must apologise for not understanding, but I would like to be clear about it.' ('I am aware', she wrote, in a comment that provokes a wry chuckle today, 'that these little books don't last long, even if they are a success.')

In the same week that she wrote, copies of Beatrix's privately printed edition were ready – Christmas presents for family and friends, the rest to be sold at a shilling each. It had gone down very well, Beatrix told Warnes a month later, adding in a postscript afterthought: 'I do not know if it is worth while mentioning – but Dr Conan Doyle 'had a copy for his children & he has a good opinion of the story & words.' Conan Doyle the creator of Sherlock Holmes, that would be. Throughout her life, the most telling part of Beatrix Potter's would very often come in a PS – a significant glimpse into her character, maybe. Witness the sting in the tail she added to a letter of May, warning Warnes that her father might be accompanying her to their offices. 'If my father happens to insist on going with me to see the agreement, would you please not mind him very much, if he is very fidgetty [sic] about things … I can of course do what I like about the book being 36.'

For an unmarried woman to be chaperoned to a place of business was not, of course, unusual in these first Edwardian days. But if anyone had tried to protest that this was merely a business relationship, then they would soon be proved wrong.

The Tailor of Gloucester was based on a story Beatrix heard while visiting the area, about a local tailor whose work was mysteriously finished for him in the night. He claimed it had been done by fairies, but in Beatrix's version the sewing was done by mice.

The member of the publishing house with whom Beatrix had most to do was Norman Warne, youngest of the three brothers now running the family company. He was also the only one unmarried, though he was a popular uncle to Harold's and Fruing's children. By July Beatrix's letters addressed to 'Dear Sir' had warmed into the more intimate (by Edwardian standards) 'Dear Mr Warne'.

Luckily they had soon plenty to talk about since Warne's first print run, 8000 copies, of *The Tale of Peter Rabbit* was already ordered before publication on 2 October. More from Miss Potter should be commissioned, clearly. In December Beatrix was sending Norman Warne 'the little book' – another which, not anticipating her commercial success, she had had printed privately. She herself would always prefer *The Tailor of Gloucester* to *Peter Rabbit*, though not all her readers would agree. 'I undertook the book with very cheerful courage, but I have not the least judgement whether it is satisfactory now that it is done,' Beatrix told Norman – and it was, she said 'most in request amongst old ladies.' This was another story that had begun life as a picture letter, to Freda Moore at Christmas 1901:

'My dear Freda,
Because you are fond of fairy tales, and have been ill, I have made you a story all for yourself – a new one that nobody has read before.
'And the queerest thing about it is – that I heard it in Gloucestershire, and that it is true – at least about the tailor, the waistcoat, and the "No more twist!"'

While visiting her cousin Caroline in Gloucestershire, Beatrix had heard a local report of a Gloucester tailor, a man called John Pritchard, who while making a suit for the mayor, for an important city occasion, left it unfinished in his workshop one night. When he returned, it was finished, all but one buttonhole – and that buttonhole was explained by a note pinned to the fabric, reading 'No more twist' (or twisted thread). Pritchard – who knew a good publicity ploy when he saw one – put it about that the work had been finished by fairies; but in Beatrix's hands it is done by grateful mice, which the Tailor has rescued from Simpkin, his cat. Beatrix transposes the story from her own day to the more romantic eighteenth century. 'I ought to make something good of the coat; I have been delighted to find I may draw some most beautiful 18th century clothes at S. Kensington museum', she wrote enthusiastically to Norman Warne.

This illustration from *The Tale of Squirrel Nutkin* (1903) shows the owl Old Brown pouncing on the impertinent Nutkin with 'a flutterment and a scufflement'.

Norman must have been impressed, as Beatrix's letters, and her ever more frequent visits to Warnes' office in Bedford Street, described the meticulous way she sourced her images, and the length of time over which she could be working on a story. A fortnight later she was writing to him from Melford Hall: 'I have been able to draw an old-fashioned fireplace here, very suitable for the tailor's kitchen.' On other visits to Gloucestershire over the years she drew records of real cottages and kitchens she could use, as well as the son of her cousin's coachman in a tailor's cross-legged pose. Once she pulled a button off her own garments in order to have an excuse to go into a tailor's shop, and observe his workings more precisely. Near the end of her life she still recalled how she had once sat 'on a door step on a blazing *hot* day' to sketch the archway into the precincts of Gloucester Cathedral, while the Tailor's shop was copied from a print of houses in old London.

Beatrix was delighted with a review in *The Tailor & Cutter*, the trade journal read by the mouse on her cover: 'we think it is by far the prettiest story connected with tailoring we have ever read'. It was always the praise of craftsmen and experts that pleased her the most. But the book does stand out from the animal stories that were to make her famous. It was not Warnes' most obvious follow-up to Peter, even were Beatrix not already committed to producing a private version before there could be

St Herbert's Island on Derwentwater provided the locale for Owl Island in *The Tale of Squirrel Nutkin*. Beatrix also made use of an American story of how squirrels 'go down the rivers on little rafts, using their tails for sails'.

any thought of a commercial one. A shortened version of *The Tailor of Gloucester* –
shorn of most of the rhymes with which Beatrix had decked her first version – was
published by Frederick Warne & Co in 1903. But so was *The Tale of Squirrel Nutkin*,
the other story on which Beatrix had been working in 1902 – another story of an
impudent small animal and a book, she said, 'more likely to appeal to people who are
accustomed to a more cheerful Christmas than I am'.

The Tale of Squirrel Nutkin could trace its roots back to that story of the squirrels who
used their tails as sails, which Beatrix had heard at Keswick in 1897 – and to a picture
letter she had sent, four years later, to Norah Moore. It was now set very clearly on
St Herbert's Island on Derwentwater, the lake on whose banks she had spent so many
summers at Lingholm. Like Peter its hero was an amiable rascal, whose teasing of
the owl Old Brown (or Mr Brown) meets with the punishment it deserved. Nutkin
escapes – but missing half his tail.

Beatrix bought two squirrels from a pet shop to use as models – though she had to
get rid of one because they fought – and refreshed her memories of Bertram's pet
owl by a visit to the Zoo. Her letters to Norman are still full of practical details,
humility about her work blended with a very clear idea of what she wanted and
strong commercial sense. (If *The Tailor* and *Squirrel Nutkin* were to be published in
two different bindings would it not be more saleable if there were clearer difference
between the two? Yes, brocade for the more expensive one as Norman had suggested,
as long as the lettering would show up on fancy cloth …) Nutkin would be one of the
first (as one might phrase it) 'authors' of the miniature letters Beatrix began sending
to some of her youthful admirers in the voices of her characters: evidence of how
vibrantly they continued to live for her long after publication day. 'Dear Sir', Squirrel
Nutkin wrote to Old Brown, in fine Edwardian phraseology: 'I should esteem it
a favour if you will let me have back my tail, as I miss it very much. I would pay
postage. yrs truly Squirrel Nutkin. An answer will oblige.'

In July 1903 she was writing to Norman 'I had been a little hoping too that something
might be said about another book'. She had plenty in 'a vague state of existence'. But
writing to Harold Warne a week later, since Norman was away on a selling trip, she
seemed to have no desire to discuss the matter with him. 'I have had such painful
unpleasantness at home this winter about the work that I should like a rest, while I
am away.' A sign, perhaps, that professional discussions with Norman Warne were
taking on a more personal significance.

Sideshows: 'Dear Mr Warne . . .'

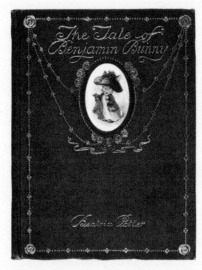

Peter Rabbit reappeared beside his cousin in *The Tale of Benjamin Bunny*.

Beatrix's other new concern at this time was a practical one – the question of what she would call her 'side-shows'; the secondary merchandise associated with the characters from her books. She was right to take it seriously. In the years and indeed the decades ahead this would prove to be a line as durable, and surely as profitable, as the books themselves. But it was also an opportunity others might easily try to exploit. In November 1903 Beatrix was writing to Norman that she had been trying her own hand at doll-making and 'cutting out patterns of Peter, I have not got it right yet, but the expression is going to be lovely; especially the whiskers'. She was anxious that Norman should get on with trying to find a manufacturer: Harrods were already selling a rabbit doll, and her father had bought a toy squirrel in the Burlington arcade advertised as 'Nutkin'. On 28 December 1903 she registered the patent for her own Peter Rabbit design. Soon would come the idea of a Peter Rabbit wallpaper, with Beatrix debating whether to accept a £10 fee from Sanderson, or whether instead to try Liberty.

These were the first tell-tale flakes in what would prove to be a positive blizzard of spin-offs from the *Tales*; and Beatrix was acutely aware of the importance of getting each new doll or china figurine right. These were, after all, ambassadors for the world of her creation. She was if anything more alive to the possibilities than were Warnes, whose failure to register *Peter Rabbit* for copyright in America had already seen the first pirated edition with many variants and unlicensed sequels to follow.

The Tale of Benjamin Bunny sees Benjamin and his cousin returning to Mr McGregor's garden to retrieve the clothes that Peter left there in his flight. They find the blue jacket and brown shoes on a scarecrow, but run into more dangerous adventures as they make their escape.

Beatrix's books for 1904 would be *The Tale of Benjamin Bunny* – which see Peter Rabbit and his cousin Benjamin return to Mr McGregor's garden to retrieve the clothes Peter lost there – and *The Tale of Two Bad Mice* (the first of what she called her 'girl's books'). The mice, Tom Thumb and his wife Hunca Munca, were drawn from two she had brought back from Gloucestershire, caught in a trap at Harescombe Grange. Beatrix's invention had them raiding a doll's house, furious to find that the tempting plates of food on the doll's table were not edible. As so often, Beatrix founded her fantasy very carefully on fact, observing Hunca Munca's behaviour with actual doll's house fittings. The mouse was 'very ready to play the game,' Beatrix wrote to Norman, despising the plaster dishes of food but captivated by anything with lace or ribbon. Beatrix's mice had needed a new cage; Norman Warne, a clever amateur carpenter, had made a marvellous doll's house for his nieces. 'I wish "Johnny Crow" would make my mouse "a little house"; do you think he would if I made a paper plan?', Beatrix asked him. 'I want one with glass at the side before I draw Hunca Munca again.' But the idea drew her into a dilemma. Beatrix had been enjoying a growing closeness with the Warne family, visiting the house in Bedford Square and beginning what would prove an enduring friendship with Norman's unmarried sister Millie, eight years older than she. But when Beatrix was invited down to the Fruing Warnes' family home in Surbiton, to see the nieces' doll's house, Beatrix's mother made difficulties. 'I should be so very sorry if Mrs Warne or you thought me uncivil,' Beatrix wrote in mortification. 'I hardly ever go out, and my mother is so "exacting" I had not enough spirit to say anything about it. I have felt vexed with myself since, but I did not know what to do. It does wear a person out.'

In March she was writing to Norman from Gwaynynog in Wales, the home of her mother's sister. 'I am also accompanied by [her pet hedgehog] Mrs Tiggy – carefully concealed – my aunt cannot endure animals!' Beatrix's first book for 1905 would be *The Tale of Mrs Tiggy-Winkle*. Four weeks later, from Lyme Regis, walking out between banks covered in primroses, she told Norman that: 'I don't know whether I shall get as far as the big land slip by myself, I have not anyone to walk with.' There was surely a message in the hints she was dropping, about how unsatisfactory she found her present life. In a PS to a letter of April, hailing the good news about *Nutkin*'s sales: 'It is pleasant to feel I could earn my own living.' That autumn, from Lingholm, she was telling that 'our summer "holiday" is always a weary business'. They were now exchanging letters almost every day.

In February of the next year she wrote to him about what would (though not immediately) become *The Tale of Mr Jeremy Fisher*: 'I'm afraid you don't like *frogs* but it would make pretty pictures with water-forget-me-nots, lilies etc.' Early in June – 'I wish another book could be planned out before the summer, if we are going on with them, I always feel very much lost when they are finished.' A fortnight later, in the postscript where her real feelings so often surfaced: 'I do so *hate* finishing books, I would like to go on with them for years.'

A talented amateur carpenter, Norman Warne made a wonderful fully furnished doll's house for his niece Winifred. Beatrix used photographs of it, and studies of her own pet mouse Hunca Munca, as models for *The Tale of Two Bad Mice* (1904).

On 21 July she wrote to Norman in distress – her beloved pet mouse was dead. 'I have made a little doll of poor Hunca Munca, I cannot forgive myself for having let her tumble. I do so miss her. She fell off the chandelier, she managed to stagger up the staircase into your little house, but she died in my hand about 10 minutes after. I think if I had broken my own neck it would have saved a deal of trouble. I should like to get some new work fixed before going to Wales.'

On 25 July, a letter about engraving and printing practicalities is as usual addressed to 'Dear Mr Warne' and signed 'I remain yrs sincerely Beatrix Potter' – but it must have crossed in the post with one from Norman, who, on that same day, wrote proposing marriage.

The Pie and the Patty-pan (1905) is about the confusion arising when a cat called Ribby invites a Pomeranian dog for tea. The book is full of recognisable glimpses of Hill Top.

There was no doubt about Beatrix's own feelings – the problem was always going to be her parents. The fact that Beatrix was now nearing 40 did not liberate her from the assumption of the day: that their approval, if not their formal consent, was required. Besides their concern about losing the daughter who would take care of them in old age, the Potters, eager to rise above their mercantile roots, were horrified that Norman Warne the publisher was 'in trade'. Beatrix was not going to be overruled by their prejudices – she told her cousin Caroline that publishing books was 'as clean a trade as spinning cotton' – and she and Norman exchanged rings. No formal announcement was to be made, however, though some of Norman's nieces were told to call Beatrix, 'Aunt Bee'.

The Tale of Mrs Tiggy-Winkle (1905) was based on Beatrix's own pet hedgehog. Even after she delivered the manuscript, she wrote to Norman's niece Winifred about the animal's doings. She always liked to write in a child's exercise book.

Before the Potter family left for their long summer holidays, to be spent this year in Wales, Beatrix had delivered not only *Mrs Tiggy-Winkle* but her second book for 1905, *The Pie and the Patty-pan*, a social comedy about a very polite tea party given for a dog by a cat. Beatrix arranged to visit the office before her departure early in August, writing to Harold, since Norman was sick: 'You will not think me very cross if I say I would rather *not* talk much yet about that business?' – her engagement – 'though I am *very glad* you have been told.

'I do trust that your brother is not going to be very ill, I got scared before he went to Manchester, wondering if he had been drinking bad water.' The secret engagement, she confessed, was 'a very awkward way of happening; I think he is going a little too fast now that he has started; but I trust it may come right in the end.' It sounds as if she could not quite believe in a happy future. Events would swiftly prove her right.

Five days after his proposal Norman, still ill, was ordered bed rest. We do not know if he and Beatrix saw each other again before she left for Wales. At this point –

significantly, perhaps – Beatrix took up the diary-writing habit again, describing the crabs and shrimps of the Welsh seaside capering hand in hand as the tide comes in. Birds, butterflies, a wood toad – these were the descriptions of the natural world in which her younger self had taken refuge. But in London, Norman was not getting any better – very cheerful, his mother noted although 'he can scarcely stand'.

His death, on 24 August, was from leukaemia; then sufficiently difficult to diagnose that no-one seems to have seen what was coming. Beatrix's holiday diary does not cover those days. But (from her later account), she had written to him the day before his death – 'a silly letter all about my rabbits, & the walking stick that I was going to get for him to thrash his wife with – but he didn't read it, so it was good enough.' She had seen a memorably beautiful evening fall in the barley field, bathed in a still grey light, a single gleam of sunshine making its way through the mist over the sea. It was the next morning when the telegram from the Warnes came, summoning her back to London to say goodbye. 'I am quite glad now I was not in time, I should only have cried & upset him', she wrote later. The Potters came back to London in time for Norman's burial in Highgate Cemetery.

Beatrix would wear Norman's ring until her death – still cherish, even, his umbrella – but she did not show her feelings indiscriminately. Her letter to Harold Warne on 5 September was mostly about the re-done proofs for *Mrs Tiggy-Winkle* – so much better than the first set 'that my dear old man was so vexed with. It will be a trying thing to come for the first time to the office, but there is no help for it. I have begun sketching again … I feel as if my work and your kindness will be my greatest comfort.'

The day after she wrote to Harold, she again sent a picture letter, this time to one of Norman's nieces – the Winifred for whom he had once made a doll's house. The Peter Rabbit Lady, as she introduced herself, wrote about gathering mushrooms, about the two bunnies she had with her in Wales, Josey and Mopsy, and the 'great traveller' Mrs Tiggy; who 'enjoys going by train', though journeys made her hungry, and who would drink milk out of a doll's tea cup if taken to Winifred's to tea.

Beatrix hoped she would write Winifred lots of letters, she told the little girl's mother at the end of the month: 'it is much more satisfactory to address a real live child; I often think that was the success of *Peter Rabbit*; it was written to a child – not made to order.' She would continue to address new tales to favoured children, and perhaps even heed their comments. Beatrix added that she and Millie had been to see Norman's grave in Highgate Cemetery – 'the stone is put back quite neatly again; it seems to want something planted at the back'. She was wondering whether white Japanese anemones would grow.

Before Christmas she sent Winifred Warne another picture letter, describing the winter slumbers of Mrs Tiggy. 'She went to sleep on Wednesday night and I don't expect her to wake up till Sunday. Did you ever hear any thing so lazy? … When I touch her she snores very loud, and curls herself up tighter.' A picture shows a hedgehog tucked up in bed, long nose just protruding from a nightcap. Perhaps Beatrix – with a cold, and a headache, 'and some nasty medicine' – wished she could hide from the world in the same way.

In was Millie to whom Beatrix revealed most of her feelings. In the spring she was in Bath, and wondering why she had accepted the invitation of relatives to stay there. She wrote to Millie of Jane Austen's final novel *Persuasion*, which was set partly in the city. Jane Austen believed Bath disagreed with her, and her heroine Anne Elliot felt that way too. *Persuasion* – the story of a woman who loses love only to find it, late, again – 'was always my favourite', Beatrix wrote, 'and I read the end part of it again last July, on the 26th, the day after I got Norman's letter. I thought my story had come right with patience and waiting like Anne Eliott's [sic] did.'

She was, she added, 'upset about poor Tiggy', who for the last fortnight had been sick and thin. 'One gets very fond of a little animal. I hope she will either get well or go quickly.' In the end she would feel the kindest thing to do was to chloroform Mrs Tiggy; but the minor loss of a loved pet at this time cannot but have reminded her painfully of the major loss.

In December she had told Millie that she was trying to think of golden sheaves and harvest – that Norman 'did not live long but he fulfilled a useful happy life. I must try to make a fresh beginning next year.' Perhaps she could already see where that new beginning would be. Beatrix had, fortunately, a new interest in the Lake District – at Hill Top in Sawrey.

Hill Top: 'something very precious to me'

Beatrix had begun negotiating to buy Hill Top farm, in the village of Near Sawrey near Esthwaite Water, before Norman's death, thanks not only to her literary earnings, but to a small legacy from the aunt with whom she had often stayed at Gwaynynog. But when she went up there in October, weeks after Norman's death, there must have been a very direct sense of using this refuge to assuage the pain of the greater comfort she had lost.

'My purchase seems to be regarded as a huge joke,' she wrote; 'I have been going over my hill with a tape measure.' The huge joke, she would discover, was that she had paid twice the price for Hill Top that a local speculator had paid only six months before – but all the business (taking the farm scales to be checked at the police station,

A view of Hill Top as Beatrix would have first known it. The growth of plants and trees means it looks very different today.

Beatrix in 1913 in the garden at Hill Top with Kep, the favourite of her collie dogs.
She wears her characteristic coat and skirt made from Herdwick tweed.

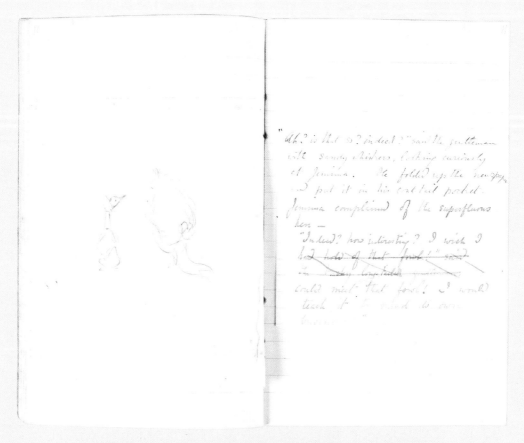

Mr Tod the fox, who made his first appearance in this manuscript for *The Tale of Jemima Puddle-Duck*, would later get his own *Tale*.

as required when a new farm owner began to trade, and laying out a new garden) must at least have brought the comfort of activity.

She could not be there for more than a few weeks a year – work, success and property were still not enough to excuse her the duties, and the constraints, of a daughter born into the Victorian age. But she needed to make decisions about the accommodation. Hill Top had been tenanted when she bought it, and Beatrix soon decided to ask the farmer, John Cannon, and his family to stay on. But she would reserve to her own use the original farmhouse with its thick walls, its 'funny cupboards & closets', and build separate accommodation for the Cannons at the side.

Like many others she found building work a more worrisome process than she had expected. She couldn't get back to Sawrey until next April and then, arriving as she wrote to Millie after a 'hot dusty journey', 'I thought my property was looking extremely ugly when I arrived I was quite glad you weren't there! The new works though doubtless an improvement are painfully new … Things very soon become moss grown at the Lakes, it will mend itself in a year or two.'

She welcomed the escape Hill Top gave her, but solitude had its perils. That summer, a visit from Gertrude Woodward having just ended, she was telling Millie: 'I should be glad if you can find time to write occasionally – even if there isn't much news to write about, it is cheering! I am going through a most awfully wet evening, & the day's newspaper has missed the post!' It was just ten days before her 40th birthday; the milestone she had hoped to spend as a married woman at last. But she was expanding her farming interests – 30 sheep, 10 cows, 14 pigs, ducks and hens, and the collie dogs she came so much to admire.

In September she was writing more cheerfully to Millie: 'There is a quarry-man who lives on the road to the ferry who has got some most splendid phloxes, they will look nice between the laurels while the laurels are small. I shall plant the lilies between the azaleas.' The locals were generous with their gifts of plants, and soon she had something from almost every house in the village. She was developing her taste for country pursuits and pleasures, attending the local harvest festival, beekeeping, gathering firewood.

Her family had been staying at Lingholm for the summer; Beatrix making the complicated, twenty mile plus, trip from Keswick to Sawrey for the day every chance she had. But she had no wish to return south when they left: 'either I will begin a cold, or the cook will give notice, or something will prevent me going back to Sawrey, and I want so much to have a good month there, to garden and get extra fat before winter.' Time and again she would write of her reluctance to leave Hill Top, writing her longing to return as she sat in London, or sat in a seaside lodging with her parents, thinking of her lambs.

Next August she was writing to Millie, 'photographing the lambs before they depart! oh Shocking! it does not do to be sentimental on a farm. I am going to have some lambskin hearthrugs.' Work continued – on the house, and on the little books. *The Tale of Mr Jeremy Fisher* had been published at last in 1906 (along with *The Story of Miss Moppet*, and *The Story of a Fierce Bad Rabbit*, less wordy books she would make for younger children and which were originally published in the panorama format of one long folding strip of paper). Jeremy Fisher had begun his life in Beatrix's

The manuscript for *The Tale of Jemima Puddle-Duck* shows Jemima outside what is clearly the porch of Hill Top, made of great stone slabs. The book is dedicated to Betsy and Ralph Cannon, the children of Hill Top's farm manager, seen collecting Jemima's eggs from the rhubarb patch.

The same view today. Beatrix said her garden was a case of survival of the fittest – 'always very full of flowers and weeds'.

imagination to the north in Scotland and to the south, where she had sketched at Melford Hall – but now he clearly lived on Esthwaite Water.

The 1907 *Tale of Tom Kitten* was set in Hill Top, and the book was dedicated 'to all Pickles – especially those that get upon my garden wall' – the gate where Tom and his siblings Mittens and Moppet perch to see the Puddle-ducks pass by. Work on the house and the books was often allied: Beatrix would say once that she could not invent, she could only copy. Of the two books published in 1908, *The Tale of Jemima Puddle-Duck* features the Hill Top gardens and the Hill Top farmer's family, Beatrix's favourite collie Kep and the hills above Sawrey. Her cousin Caroline remembers going around with her looking for a suitable spot for Jemima to make her nest.

The previous autumn Beatrix had been writing to Millie: 'Another room has been got straight, the front kitchen – or hall – as I call it. I have not meddled with the fireplace, I don't dislike it, and besides it is wanted for the next book.' This is the fireplace featured in the book Beatrix first called *The Roly-Poly Pudding*, though it was later renamed *The Tale of Samuel Whiskers*. The book is full of glimpses of the house at Hill Top, from the hall, the half landing, and the clock, right down to the very curtains. 'Farmer Potatoes', the neighbour plagued by rats in the book, is taken directly from a photograph of Beatrix's neighbour John Postlethwaite; while the rats make their way through the gaps in the thick walls, up the chimney and under the floorboards, just as they did at the real Hill Top.

This book sees naughty Tom Kitten once again in trouble, captured by the 'dreadful 'normous big rat' Samuel Whiskers and rolled up in pastry ready to be baked as a pudding. Though Samuel Whiskers and his wife Anna Maria are the villains here, the book's dedication reads: 'In Remembrance of "Sammy", The Intelligent pink-eyed Representative of a Persecuted (but Irrepressible) Race. An Affectionate little Friend, and most accomplished thief.' Beatrix long remembered the white rat she had kept as a pet. 'I have memory of him waddling along the floor, wanting to be picked up by my Aunt … always wanting to be petted in his declining months … I remember the Aunt providing a hard boiled egg, and watching the rolling of the egg along a passage, but she requested that his nest box might be kept firmly fastened.'

Left Samuel Whiskers with the rolling pin he will use to make Tom Kitten into a pudding.
Right The landing at Hill Top still looks very much the same today.

Norman Warne had been sceptical when Beatrix first suggested *The Tale of Mr Jeremy Fisher* (1906). 'I'm afraid you don't like frogs but it would make pretty pictures with water-forget-me-nots, lilies etc.,' she wrote.

But bunnies were still the big seller – 'all the little boys and girls like the rabbits best', she told one young admirer. As 1908 turned to 1909 Beatrix was working on *The Tale of the Flopsy Bunnies*, the charming misadventures of Benjamin Bunny's offspring, still thwarting the evil designs of Mr McGregor. This time the garden was taken from the one at Gwaynynog, which Beatrix had described almost fifteen years before – 'very productive but not tidy, the prettiest kind of garden, where bright old fashioned flowers grow amongst the currant bushes'. Her next book would be set even closer to home. *The Tale of Ginger and Pickles*, which came out the same year, is set in the Sawrey village shop, now kept by Ginger the yellow tomcat and Pickles the terrier, and frequented by characters from Beatrix's other books, from Peter Rabbit to Mrs Tiggy-winkle. It is dedicated to a bedridden old man of the village, dubbed John Dormouse, who had wanted to be in one of Beatrix's books, but unfortunately died before this one appeared.

The shop sells 'red spotted pocket-handkerchiefs at a penny three farthings', as well as sugar and snuff, and galoshes. Today the book is notable for its picture of life in a world gone by, and indeed of market economy. Ginger and Pickles's habit of giving unlimited credit finally puts them out of business, unable to pay their tax bill. This in turn allows their competitor Tabitha Twitchit, Tom Kitten's mother, to put up her prices. But to the inhabitants of Sawrey its charm lay elsewhere. In November 1909 Beatrix was writing to Millie: 'The "Ginger & Pickle" book has been causing

Left The Puddle-ducks in *The Tale of Tom Kitten* in front of what is now the Buckle Yeat Guest House (right), just one of the real Near Sawrey buildings featured in the story.

amusement, it has got a good many views which can be recognized in the village which is what they like, they are all quite jealous of each others [sic] houses & cats getting into a book.'

Cat and dog, living up to their animal natures, have some difficulty in refraining from eating their customers – Ginger cannot bear, he says, 'to see them going out at the door carrying their little parcels'. But it was after *Ginger and Pickles* came out that Beatrix wrote to the owner of the real, distinctively coloured 'Ginger', in a rare expression of dissatisfaction with the animal world she portrayed: 'it is an unfortunate fact that animals in their own natural pretty fur coats don't sell so well as dressed – and one has to consider the bills at this time of year'.

The Tale of Ginger and Pickles caused a lot of discussion among Beatrix's neighbours, all wondering whether their pet had been pictured in the book.

Indeed, one element of the juggling act Beatrix was forced to perform in these years was the fact that she needed money from her invented animals for the farm and her real ones. But the truth was she was always juggling – juggling her time. Most of the year was still spent in London with her ageing parents, and even the months in the Lake District with her family saw difficulties in getting away to Sawrey for the day. 'It is awkward with old people, especially in winter – it is not very fit to leave them.' Even when she was at Hill Top it was a tussle whether to spend time on her farming activities, or on filling her sketchbook for the next year's publications.

Beatrix could and did conduct some of her operations from Bolton Gardens, and in 1910 she was in London when she commissioned a leaflet protesting against the government's horse census (which triggered fears the horses could be commandeered by the army). 'It must not be let out the horse leaflet is written by a *female*. I should give it away as written by a small farmer in Lancashire,' she said. From Bolton Gardens, too, she could speak out on another of the causes that made her play an unwontedly active part in the run up to the 1910 election. The issue was that of free trade. Beatrix had long been incensed to find that her soft toys had to be manufactured abroad, since the free-trade rules had seen the British toy trade, once centred on London's Camberwell district, killed off by cheap foreign imports. Now she wanted not free, but fair, trade, she said. 'I am so busy over the Election, my fingers are quite stiff with drawing posters.'

In its quiet way, this was rebellion. Beatrix's family had strong links to the free trade cause. But she was becoming less ready to be bound by old ties – concerned about Harold Warne's dilatory approach to business and to the merchandising of her creations. 'I must ask you *not to make any fresh arrangements* without letting me know, I am seriously provoked about things being in such a muddle', read the postscript of one letter to him in the spring of 1910. On another, 'I must confess I sometimes regret the times when cheques were smaller but *punctual*'. Though Beatrix was making real money now, not least from the spin-offs she called her 'side shows', this was a foreshadow of trouble in years ahead.

Her family were problematic too, her father's health making him ever more irritable; Bolton Gardens was ever summoning her back. From Hill Top, she was still writing to Millie: 'I hope I may be able to stop till the end of the week, I was much wanting a change, it has been rather a trying season.' The following year she was writing to Millie of her doings on the Sawrey coronation celebration committee – she was 'a determined person, but – unfortunately non-resident'.

The books were coming at the rate only of one a year now, and they were not necessarily her best. 1910's *The Tale of Mrs Tittlemouse* saw a houseproud mouse plagued by a host of messy visitors, from the toad Mr Jackson to Babbitty Bumble the bee. 1911 saw *Peter Rabbit's Painting Book*, with its famous admonition 'Don't put the Brush in your mouth. If you do, you will be ill, like Peter'; and *The Tale of Timmy Tiptoes*, in which Beatrix uncharacteristically tried to please her US audience with the story of a grey squirrel, a chipmunk and even a black bear – animals with which she did not have her usual familiarity.

There was perhaps a sense of letting off steam in her campaign of 1912, one which brought her, as so often, shoulder to shoulder with Hardwicke Rawnsley. She wrote indignantly to Millie of 'a beastly fly-swimming spluttering aeroplane careering up & down over Windermere; it makes a noise like 10 million bluebottles.' Her public letters and her petitions, had their effect, and the flying machine disappeared.

The same year saw the publication of *The Tale of Mr Tod*; but this was once again a tale she had conceived some time before, a story that ties up the Flopsy Bunnies with Jemima Puddle-duck, as Benjamin Bunny's children are kidnapped by Brock the badger and almost wind up as dinner for the fox Mr Tod. The book would appeal to boys for the long fight between fox and badger, and perhaps for its promise of 'dreadful bad language', but Beatrix was annoyed with Harold Warne's timorous suggestions for change to this darker, and longer, story.

'If it were not impertinent to lecture ones [sic] publisher – you are a great deal too much afraid of the public for whom I have never cared one tuppeny-button. I am sure that it is that attitude of mind which has enabled me to keep up the series. Most people, after one success, are so cringingly afraid of doing less well that they rub all the edge off their subsequent work.' It had been a dreadful summer, complicated by an outbreak of foot-and mouth disease; she was exhausted; it all 'takes it out of me', she wrote to Millie. But perhaps she saw escape ahead.

You will want a Brush
and 5 Paints ———
Antwerp Blue
Crimson Lake
Gamboge
Sap Green and
Burnt Sienna

You can mix
Blue with the Sienna
to make dark Brown.
Don't put the Brush in your
mouth. If you do, you will be
ill, like Peter.

The instructions at the front of *Peter Rabbit's Painting Book* warned children not to put the brush in their mouths, or they would be ill like Peter, who eats too many vegetables from Mr McGregor's patch, and has to be put to bed with a dose of chamomile tea.

In 1909 Beatrix had bought Castle Farm in Sawrey, whose farmhouse, Castle 'Cottage' looked across a meadow to Hill Top. She had in fact, over the years, been steadily buying up parcels of land around the village. Each purchase brought her into further contact with the Hawkshead solicitors who did the work for her, W.H. Heelis and Son – and with William Heelis, almost five years younger than she.

Amiable, sporting, the youngest of eleven children, William was deeply attached to the Lakes and Westmorland where he had grown up. He had given Beatrix advice on her purchases and her improvements – and in June 1912 he asked her to marry him. Once again her feelings were clear but her position was not: her parents were no more likely to accept William than they had been Norman. Not only was he in their eyes a poor match, but the son of an Anglican rector. And with her father now 80, a daughter's duty of care was not easily put aside.

She was ill that winter, with a flu that turned to bronchial pneumonia, and whose effects went on for months. 'I have been resting on my back for a week as my heart has been rather disturbed by the Influenza. I am assured it will recover with quiet.' But by April she was still telling Harold Warne that, 'I seem to get on very slowly, I am decidedly stronger & look perfectly well, but I was completely stopped by a short hill on trying to walk to the next village this afternoon.' Perhaps in some way, her very illness moved things on.

Beatrix's cousin Caroline – who had preached independence to her once before – advised her to marry William quietly, whatever her parents said. Beatrix herself was increasingly aware that she was 'best out of London', whether or not her parents were determined to remain.

Now Beatrix's brother loyally entered the fray. For more than a decade he had been living as a farmer and landscape painter in the Scottish borders – now he revealed that he had also, unknown to his parents though perhaps not to Beatrix, been living as a married man. Perhaps the news of what Bertram's parents would consider his misalliance made Beatrix's plan more acceptable. By the time the Potters went to spend the summer at Lindeth Howe, on Windermere, some accommodation seemed to have been achieved.

Castle Cottage, just across a meadow from Hill Top, was where Beatrix and William Heelis actually lived. When Beatrix married she simply locked the door on her old home, leaving it fully furnished as her writing retreat.

Beatrix and William were engaged. She was free now to let people know – particularly the Warnes, and Millie. 'I have felt very uncomfortable and guilty when with you for some time – especially when you asked about Sawrey. You would be only human if you felt a little hurt! Norman was a saint, if ever man was good, I do not believe he would object, especially as it was my illness and the miserable feeling of loneliness that decided me at last.'

Millie wrote with warm reassurance: this was indeed what Norman would have wished. But the Potters were holding out for the actual marriage being postponed, and Beatrix clearly feared that this tomorrow would never come. At one point, she was even afraid the engagement might, 'for the time', be broken off. As they returned to London in late September Beatrix was, she wrote to Gertrude Woodward, 'tempted to bolt at once'. She 'was feeling the going away very much' – but William 'has actually been invited up for a weekend soon – they never say much but they cannot dislike him.' Firmly, now, she told her cousin Fanny that: 'I am going to get married!'

'They like him now they have got over the shock, & he is very nice with old people & anxious to be friendly & useful … He is 42 (I am 47) very quiet – dreadfully shy, but I'm sure he will be more comfortable married … He is in every way satisfactory, well known in the district and respected.' Her parents' opposition had 'only made us more fond of one another'.

'We have every prospect of happiness – if it pleases Heaven,' she wrote. But – remembering, no doubt, what had happened before – she wished 'to get it over, I don't seem to believe in it'. This time, however, she would be wrong to worry.

On 15 October, at the Potter's neighbourhood church of St Mary Abbot's in Kensington, Helen Beatrix Potter and William Heelis were married, the marriage witnessed by her parents and Gertrude Woodward. The day before the wedding Rupert Potter took a photograph of the bridal pair. They returned to Sawrey for a short honeymoon, collecting a white bull at the station in Windermere.

To Millie, Beatrix sent a cutting of the announcement and a note: 'I am sending you belated cake, which I hadn't the courage to do before! … I am *very* happy, & in every way satisfied with Willie – It is best now not to look back. But I can assure you I shall *always* remain yrs very aff. Beatrix Heelis.'

Her name was not the only thing that was different, now. Once Beatrix had dreaded finishing every book. In the weeks before her wedding, by contrast, she was adding an afterthought on a letter to Gertrude – 'I only got rid of the revised proofs [of *The Tale of Pigling Bland*] last week, it is disgracefully late, it has been such a nuisance all summer.' It was an important sign of another great change to come.

The Potters had always opposed their daughter's marrying, but when eventually Beatrix did marry William Heelis on 15 October 1913, the occasion was marked with a studio portrait.

Pigling Bland

The Tale of Pigling Bland (1913) came out within weeks of Beatrix's marriage to William Heelis. It would prove to mark a significant break in her publishing career.

Beatrix wrote 'I enclose the pig story' to Harold Warne in the spring of 1913. 'I think it is rather pretty; but I cannot say how it may strike other people.' Beatrix Potter always denied that there was any autobiographical element in *The Tale of Pigling Bland*. A few weeks after the book came out – and a few weeks after she was married – she wrote to one young admirer, who had sent congratulations: 'The portrait of two pigs arm in arm – looking at the sun-rise is not a portrait of me & Mr Heelis, though it is a view of where we used to walk on Sunday afternoons! When I want to put William in a book – it will have to be as some very tall thin animal.' But generations of readers have questioned her denial, without even knowing that as an engagement present for Norman Warne Beatrix had drawn Cinderella's carriage. Drawn, that is, the story of an escape.

'I think I shall put *myself* in the next book, it will be about pigs', she had written to a child in New Zealand, at the beginning of 1910. Indeed, Beatrix is a presence in the *Tale* from the start, scolding the mother of a family of naughty piglets. 'Aunt Pettitoes,

Aunt Pettitoes! You are a worthy person, but your family is not well brought up.' Six of the eight piglets have been in mischief, and Beatrix 'whipped them myself and led them out by the ears. Cross-patch tried to bite me'. She agrees when Aunt Pettitoes declares they must be sent away, since there will be more to eat without them. Beatrix had written in much the same terms in a letter from her farm a few years before: 'The two biggest little pigs have been sold, which takes away from the completeness of the family group. But they have fetched a good price, and their appetites were fearful – 5 meals a day and not satisfied.'

When Pigling Bland and his brother set out for market, is it ever quite clear whether they are going to hire themselves out, or to be sold, and fattened for meat? Animals in Beatrix Potter stories frequently go into a new situation unsure whether they are

Pigling Bland meets the 'perfectly lovely little black Berkshire pig', Pig-wig, who – less naive than Pigling himself – knows she has been stolen for bacon or ham.

going to be befriended, or eaten. (Any shy person, of course – and Beatrix was shy – has often felt the same way.) By the same token, when Pigling Bland meets the pretty little black pig called Pig-wig, she makes no bones about the fact that she has been stolen for bacon or hams, adding cheerfully that she plans to escape.

Beatrix had herself in her early days at Hill Top made a pet of one little black piglet who she kept it in a basket by her bed and bottle fed. She later wrote of 'Aunt Susan' who liked being tickled under the chin, and nibbled Beatrix's galoshes. But that didn't mean, as she grew into farming life, that she would be sentimental about the breed as a whole. 'I had lately a pig that continually stood on its hindlegs leaning over the pig stye, but it's hanging up, unphotographed & cured now', she would write a few years ahead.

But there are more fundamental connections between *The Tale of Pigling Bland* and Beatrix's own life. She had after all been working on the book at the time of decision about her future with William. As Pigling Bland is told: 'if you once cross the county

The signpost at which Pigling gazes on the cover of the first edition could reflect the turning point in Beatrix's own life. It can still be seen in the lanes below Near Sawrey

Beatrix always denied that the illustration of Pigling Bland and Pig-wig watching the sun rise represented herself and William – but many since have made the connection.

boundary you cannot come back.' Pigling Bland and Pig-wig are shown walking past a signpost at a crossroads – a place where you have to choose your way. This signpost is clearly the one just below the village of Near Sawrey, under Hill Top. Beatrix had earlier made a watercolour of it; she and William used to walk by the place, which still looks very much the same today. After many adventures Pigling Bland and Pig-wig escape 'over the hills and far away' – and now Beatrix too was free.

The world of Sawrey is seen time and again in the book. The very grocer with his cart and horse, who tries to pick up the pigs, is carefully copied from a photograph Beatrix had taken. But *Pigling Bland* was far from the only book of which this was true. *The Tale of Ginger and Pickles* is set in the Sawrey village shop; the fox and badger in *The Tale of Mr Tod* live very specifically in the hills above the village – 'at the top of Bull Banks, under Oatmeal Crag' – while *The Tale of Samuel Whiskers* and of course *The Tale of Tom Kitten* are pictured in Hill Top itself. Beatrix always wrote to her often-youthful correspondents in a way that made little distinction between fantasy and reality – of how Mr Tod and Tommy Brock were still fighting, of how Mr Samuel Whiskers must have been to call, since a strip of her closet wallpaper had been gnawed away … Perhaps it is Beatrix's sheer conviction that ensures her books still speak to us today.

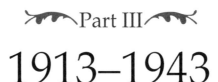

Part III

1913–1943

Mrs Heelis: 'A Woman Farmer'

On 28 October, from Hill Top Farm, Beatrix was writing: 'I am going to London this next week, Thursday, as my mother is changing servants. It is rather soon to have to leave the disconsolate Wm. People are sure to say we have quarrelled!' The letter was signed Beatrix Heelis – the name by which she would henceforth insist on being known. From London she wrote that she felt 'very dumpy' without her husband. The marriage was and would remain a success.

She felt she was putting her old life behind her. Among her things in Bolton Gardens she found a packet of Norman's letters, but could not bear to go through them. She told his sister Millie that she felt she now 'scarcely ought' to be keeping his such personal mementos as his pipe. But in fact Norman would continue to occupy a place distinct from William's in her heart – just as his ring did, now on her right hand.

The rituals of their first months of marriage were those of any other new couple. Settling into temporary accommodation while their new home of Castle Cottage was made ready, learning to cook (roasts and veg – William tried his hand at pastry), going to William's old home at Appleby for Beatrix to meet his family. Less usual is the fact that at the very end of this extraordinary year, Beatrix completed the purchase of another 66 acres to add to her little queendom at Sawrey, including the Moss Eccles Tarn on Claife Heights, which she stocked with waterlilies and with trout for William, the fisherman.

But the new year brought troubles private and public. Her father's health had continued to worsen, necessitating Beatrix's frequent return to London, and on 8 May he died. Beatrix was relieved he was free from his 'miserable state', but exhausted. 'I choke & cough, and Wm hops out of bed & applies all manner of poultices and pilasters'. Just three months later came the outbreak of the Great War.

The war perhaps reinforced Beatrix's instinctive movement away from London – and even from publishing. She settled her mother in a cottage in Sawrey, where she seemed 'wonderfully contented', though later she would move to the larger house of Lindeth Howe. Beatrix had that spring done some work on a new story, *The Tale of Kitty-in-Boots*, but had been, she wrote to Harold Warne in the summer 'a good deal damped by neither you nor Fruing seeming to care much for the story … It is very difficult to keep up to a fixed level of success.' This book would not be published until 2016 and, for the first time in twelve years, Christmas 1913 came and went without a new Beatrix Potter tale. The farm was itself a challenge, with the fear that farm horses would be conscripted, and many of the local 'lads' gone away – too many of them to be killed in the disaster of Gallipoli.

Beatrix had purchased various parcels of property around Hill Top, including Moss Eccles Tarn on Claife Heights, which she stocked with trout and waterlilies. She and William would sometimes take out a rowing boat there.

William Heelis fostered Beatrix's interest in the traditional country pursuits of the Lake District. Here he is seen country dancing – though Beatrix was more likely just to watch.

There were still 'mild dissipations' she and William could share, like the two dances they hosted for local children and farm workers. William was an enthusiastic country dancer, and Beatrix loved to look on. But one thing she did not feel able to share with William was her troubles with the Warne publishing company.

Beatrix had for several years been concerned about the lack, less of regular payment of her royalties than of information. In May 1915 she wrote that: 'I have thought once or twice I must really say I don't like going on indefinitely without some sort of accounts'. The last she could find were from 1911! By December: 'I am not out of temper; I am very sorry for you all, in the struggle that you must be having. But I am tired of the muddle, and it is *not* all due to the war.'

Small wonder she was less than enthusiastic about continuing to produce more work for them. She had tried a little drawing in the winter 'but could not stick to it, also could not see, my eyes are gone so long sighted & not clear nearby'. It was becoming ever more difficult to get the farm work done. But a letter Beatrix wrote to *The Times* in March 1916 brought unexpected dividends. Writing as 'A Woman Farmer', she declared herself happy to hire 'the right sort' of woman to do land work; and was promptly contacted by a former governess, 'Louie' Choyce, offering her services.

'Do you mind telling me, are you a girl or middle-aged?', Beatrix wrote in reply. 'I am fifty this year – very active and cheerful … My husband is a solicitor; as there are all sorts of people in the world I may say he is a very quiet gentleman, and I am a total abstainer! … I have poultry, orchard, flower garden, vegetables, no glass, help with heavy digging, cooking with the girl's assistance. Mrs C., I and this girl [the wife of the Hill Top farmer John Cannon, and the one servant at Castle Cottage] all help with hay, and I single turnips when I can find time … I don't go out much, haven't time; and the little town seems nothing but gossip and cards … I am very downright, but I get on with everybody'. And as if to prove the last point, Beatrix added after the signature: 'Your letter is very earnest: I wonder if you have a sense of humour?' In fact Miss Choyce was to become a lifelong friend, writing that 'I simply do like Mrs Heelis extraordinarily', and adding that Beatrix and William 'believe together in the simple life'.

The next year Beatrix wrote to a child in New Zealand, describing the inhabitants of her farm – or those still left to her in war time: 'an old shepherd, 2 boys & 2 girls; a

Beatrix in the garden at Hill Top, photographed by her father in May 1913, five months before her marriage.

When in 1917 Frederick Warne's were putting pressure on Beatrix to produce another book, she wondered whether it 'would be too shabby' to put together some old drawings as *Appley Dapply's Nursery Rhymes* (1917). She had made the mice sketches years before to illustrate 'There was an old woman who lived in a shoe'.

black white dog, a pony called Dolly, 3 horses, 14 cows, a lot of calves & young cattle, and 80 ewes & 40 young sheep & some pigs & 25 hens & 5 ducks, & there were 13 turkeys.' The fox had got most of the birds but there were plenty of rabbits – both pets and for pies – a cat, and, she said, at times 'Tom Kittens'.

In March 1917 she was writing to Harold Warne that her ploughman had been called up in the middle of ploughing, and the stormy weather saw wet lambs being put to dry before the fire – 'the third dead since breakfast has just expired!' But a few more weeks saw an end to such chatty communications. At the beginning of April, Harold was arrested for fraud, accused of passing £20,000 worth of forged bills, and diverting money from the publishing house into a failing fishing company he had inherited.

Beatrix's first reaction was a rush of warm sympathy towards the women of the family, her friends, and towards Fruing who was not in any way implicated. Her second was to keep William out of it, for he might not understand – 'I don't mean that he is a hard man,' she wrote to Millie, 'but he is so different to Norman.'

The year before, she had assured Harold that: 'It is unthinkable that I should ever quarrel with you and your family.' They were after all Norman's family; and as Harold was sentenced to eighteen months hard labour in Wormwood Scrubs, Beatrix set about doing all she could to help Fruing, the sole remaining brother, rescue the company. In June she told Fruing that she found she could 'scrape together' sufficient old drawings to make a small book, and *Appley Dapply's Nursery Rhymes* was published for Christmas 1917. *Tom Kitten's Painting Book,* and a revised *Peter Rabbit* one, helped with funds. She wrote to Fruing Warne: 'I can't wish anybody a very happy Christmas, but when things are worst they usually mend.'

But the books were now an effort for her. On 4 May 1918 'I am sending you 6 drawings – in desperation – I simply cannot see to put colour in them' she wrote

The Tale of Johnny Town-Mouse (1918) explores the rival charms of town and country life. Here, country mouse Timmy Willie finds himself at a dinner party of long-tailed town mice – eight courses, 'not much of anything, but truly elegant'.

The manuscript of *Johnny Town-Mouse*, which Beatrix concluded with a statement of her own feeling: 'For my part I prefer to live in the country, like Timmy Willie.'

on the eve of a creditors' meeting. The book that came out in 1918, *The Tale of Johnny Town-Mouse*, expressed her own feelings. In a story which pitted the pleasures of town life against those of the country, Beatrix on the last page placed herself firmly in the camp of country mouse Timmy Willie.

The sudden death of her brother that summer, the ever-mounting pressure on Britain's farmers and the fear lest William might be called up, all obscured pleasure in the fact that the war was coming to an end. Fruing's urging was now a pressure for her. 'Somehow when one is up to the eyes in work with real live animals it makes one despise paper-book-animals – but I mustn't say that to my publisher!', she had written, coming in off the hills after 'a rough two hours' searching for some sheep. In 1919 she told him firmly that: 'you must not count on my going on doing books of coloured illustrations. Find someone else.'

In November: 'I am glad you are having a good season – apart from my misdeeds – which you will have to put up with sooner or later – for you don't suppose I shall be able to continue these d … d little books when I am dead and buried!! I am utterly tired of doing them and my eyes are wearing out. I will try to do you one or two more for the good of the old firm; but it is quite time I had a rest from them.' She signed off 'with kind regards and very moderate apologies'.

Letter after letter harps on the same theme: 'after all I have done about 30 books, so I have earned a holiday'. In 1921 she was writing ever more sharply to Fruing Warne: 'You have got to understand sooner or later that my eyes are nothing like they used to be, and that persistent worrying me to strain them is not very kind.'

Beatrix was always actively concerned with the merchandising that accompanied her books – particularly the china, like this Grimwades Peter Rabbit-patterned children's ware.

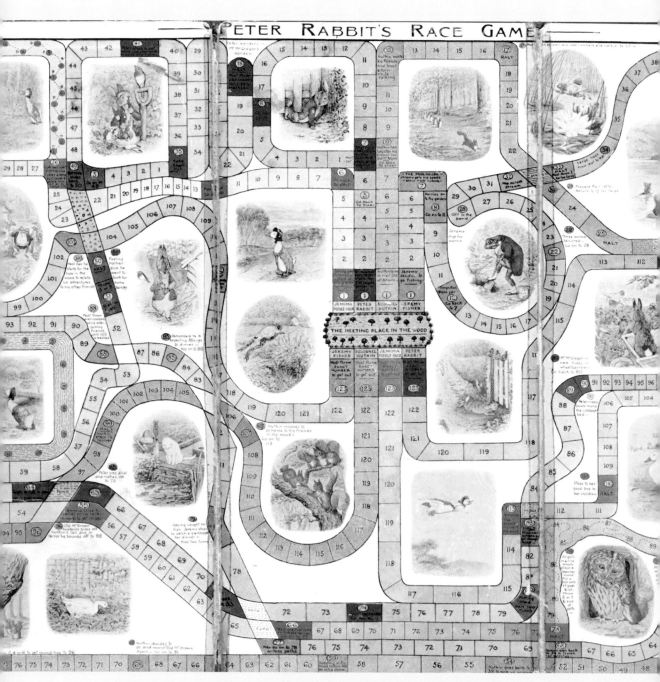

Peter Rabbit also spawned a board game which pitted four of her characters against each other.

Not that she had in any sense lost touch with her characters. She was still passionately concerned with the marketing of them – returning time and again to the subject of china, in particular, both figurines and nursery tea sets, and wishing to replace the German manufacturer with the English Grimwades. By the 1920s, besides the soft toys there were also handkerchiefs, slippers, specially made book cases and packets of children's stationery. Beatrix was also talking to Fruing's wife Mary about the best version of a board game. She would manage – galvanised by a new development in her life, a stream of American visitors enthusiastic about her work – to find drawings in her portfolios from which to make *Cecily Parsley's Nursery Rhymes* for Christmas 1922. She would continue to engage in a kind of dialogue with her child correspondents, joyful accomplices in the blurring of fact and fantasy, sending letters from or reports about the latest doings of her characters in a way which shows they were still alive in her mind.

But her real life now lay well away from the publishing industry.

Community: 'through many changing seasons'

Any visitor to the area near Sawrey today will notice the panda-striped 'belted Galloway' cattle – black, with a white belt around their middle. The Galloway breed was the one which Beatrix preferred. They'll also see grey sheep with white faces, whose lambs are born jet black and turn first chocolate, then pale. Herdwick sheep, the breed on which Beatrix Potter became an expert, and for which she was a passionate crusader.

Herdwicks are a hardy breed, able to endure harsh winters and poor vegetation – able, even, to survive many days buried under snowdrifts, eating their own lanolin-rich fleece. They have moreover the instinct of 'heafing', or hefting – remaining drawn to a particular patch of pasture, which means they can safely be left unfenced

The illustrations for *Cecily Parsley's Nursery Rhymes* (1922) reflected the country life Beatrix so valued. These rabbits are clearly enjoying the 'good ale' that brown rabbit Cecily Parsley brewed for gentlemen.

Beatrix's drawing of the guinea-pigs' garden in *Cecily Parsley's Nursery Rhymes* accompanied a rhyme by her friend Louie Choyce.

and unsupervised on the high fells. Their rough wool and comparatively poor lambing record mean they have little widespread commercial appeal, but they were ideal for the district in which Beatrix had made her home. She would be known for her suits of Herdwick wool.

The interest in Herdwick sheep was one of the concerns Beatrix shared with Hardwicke Rawnsley. Both saw the Herdwicks as part of the life and legacy of the hill farms, part of the Lake District they were so concerned to preserve. In 1895 Rawnsley, with the housing reformer Octavia Hill and the leading lawyer Sir Robert Hunter, had been one of the three founders of the National Trust – or, to give its full name, The National Trust for Places of Historic Interest or Natural Beauty. But when Rawnsley died in 1920, it was up to Beatrix to take a more active role in carrying on his work.

This, unlike her books, was a field of interest she could share with William, whose family were woven into the Lakeland community in a way Beatrix, as a newcomer, could never be. It was William who, in 1923, alerted Beatrix that Troutbeck Park Farm was up for sale – an area of fell a few miles to the east of Ambleside – and who helped her to outbid the developers who had hoped to use it for holiday homes. Today, of course, it seems extraordinary that such a thing might ever have been allowed, looking at the majesty of Troutbeck Tongue – 'uncanny, a place of silences and whispering echoes', Beatrix wrote later, 'a mighty table-land between two streams'. She moved fast to save it.

The initial purchase was of almost two thousand acres, at a price of £8000. But over the next four years Beatrix would spend another £4000 on the parcels of land nearby which would preserve its magic, ensuring that there could never be even the 'one red tiled bungalow' there. The scheme she revealed in almost weekly letters exchanged with the new secretary of the National Trust, S. H. Hamer, was a typically careful and detailed one. It would never be possible for one individual to purchase huge tracts of the Lakes, but by – for example, at Troutbeck – purchasing all the land along the roads which formed the area's outer boundary, she could ensure that without access, the whole place was problematic for developers.

Left In 1923 Beatrix purchased Troutbeck Park Farm, with the idea of bequeathing it to the National Trust. She wrote of 'the wonderful view over Troutbeck Tongue, and blue shadows creeping up the head of the den'.
Above Troutbeck Farm interior. Beatrix was as concerned to preserve the farmhouse as the dramatic landscape.

Beatrix became an impassioned supporter and breeder of the tough, free-ranging Herdwick sheep.

Beatrix always intended that Troutbeck should go to the National Trust after her death, but she hoped to live long enough to put the run-down Troutbeck Farm on a sounder footing. She wanted to plant larches, and to build up the stock of 'pure bred heafed Herdwicks'. Too many of the sheep already on site were 'rotten' with the parasite liver fluke; the streams polluted and the barns beset with cannibalistic rats. Even the old farm house was run down.

Setting about the clean-up operation Beatrix reserved one room in the farmhouse for herself (where, with a microscope, she would check the sheep's dung for the dreaded parasites). But she brought in a farm manager and also a head shepherd, Tom Storey, whose wage she doubled to lure him into her employ, and who would remain a trusted ally. Soon Beatrix asked him to move to Hill Top, where she wanted to start showing Herdwick sheep. When her lambs won first prize, for the first time, she was 'as proud as a dog with two tails'. They had occasional disputes but Beatrix, Tom said, was prepared to bow to real superior knowledge, and, of course, to learn. A decade or so after she first expanded her farming concerns with Troutbeck, she was expert enough to be called as a show judge of Herdwick sheep – and of sheepdogs.

Also working at Troutbeck – hired each year for the lambing season – was Joe Moscrop, another shepherd who would stick by Beatrix until her dying day. As she wrote one year, later in their acquaintance, 'it wouldn't be like lambing time without Joseph and *his dog*. I am expecting that the remuneration will include the four footed assistant again.' Another time she would be writing to ask whether he was already fixed with a lambing dog, and if not, might he use her own Lassie – no 'useless favourite', but keen and obedient, and 'very gentle with sheep. She is still a

COCKERMOUTH AND DISTRICT AGRICULTURAL SOCIETY.

ANNUAL SHOW,
21st September, 1933.

CHAMPION

HERDWICK FEMALE.

J. JACKSON, Secretary.
R. BOUSTEAD, Asst. Secretary.

LOWESWATER & BRACKENTHWAITE
AGRICULTURAL SOCIETY

Annual Show, Thursday, 16th Sept., 1937

CHAMPION
(Given by H. W. Ainsworth, Esq.)

Best Herdwick (Female)

Loweswater and Brackenthwaite
AGRICULTURAL SOCIETY.

ANNUAL SHOW, - - 1938

CHAMPION

Best Herdwick (Female)

Beatrix often showed her sheep. The first time she won first prize her shepherd Tom Storey (pictured above with Beatrix in the background) said she was 'as proud as a dog with two tails'. A decade later, in 1936, Beatrix could tell a friend 'The sheep got many prizes, but not so many as the previous year.'

bit inclined to bunch flock at a distance and sit down. I expect she will get out of that at Troutbeck … '

She still wrote about her animals with huge affection but lack of sentiment. 'I shall be glad to get the turkeys safely off, & the horrid slaughter over, poor dears they are so tame and tractable, but they *do* eat.' But she wrote also with humour, telling a child in the US: 'I heard a noise just now like somebody talking in the kitchen – there was Mr Drake Puddleduck and 6 Mrs Ducks *sitting* on the *mat* before the *kitchen fire*!! … Had it been hens, or turkeys, I should not have been surprised.' She would have kennels built for old working dogs at Troutbeck – animals past their usefulness – as many as 14 of them at one time.

To the uninitiated, Beatrix's letters to Joseph Moscrop about farm matters read almost as if they were in code, like her diary. Letters about 'hilling heifers' and their 'board teeth', about a mare's being 'laid in' and 'early bite' in the fields. (Many of Beatrix's commands about her farms hardly make sense unless you know that 'gimmer hogs', for example, mean young female sheep and 'gimmer twinters' those of two winters.) But her letters to Joe Moscrop were also joky, bickering about his price. 'But you will please come down a pound Joseph – take it or leave it!', she wrote on one occasion.

Ulla Hyde Parker recalled that as she went around with Beatrix, visiting the farms she owned, they 'were greeted with respect but perhaps not much warmth. Mrs Heelis, as she was always called and referred to, was very much their superior.' Brusque rather than chatty – with the staff in William's office, for example – she did not make friends everywhere. Ulla quickly realised 'that her tenants stood in some awe of her; but when we reached her various shepherds, guarding large flocks of sheep, she would jump quickly out of the car, and with these men there was immediate contact, for she and they understood one another'.

'Tant' Benson who replaced Tom Storey at Troutbeck recalled how, when she made her regular visit to pay his wages, she would always give the money to his wife, not to him. In seventeen years 'she never paid me once. She always gave the money to the missus … "That's where it should be," she would say, "for the housekeeping."'

Beatrix had taken several steps into involvement with the local community. She was instrumental in getting Hawkshead its own District Nurse (an innovation she herself found of use when offering a home, for several years, to William's invalid brother). And she allowed troops of Guides to camp in her fields, through William's sister who led the Hawkshead pack. This last gave her a particular pleasure, allowing her 'to understand and share the joy of life that is being lived by the young'. It was, she acknowledged, exactly the kind of youthful communal experience her own childhood had lacked.

In later years Beatrix often allowed Girl Guides to camp on her land, and loved to join them.

In 1927 Beatrix invoked the help of her American readers in a crusade to save Cockshott Point on Lake Windermere, which was threatened with town extension.

In 1927 Beatrix joined the National Trust campaign to preserve Cockshott Point, a strip of foreshore near the Windermere Ferry, from development. And when the public subscription showed signs of falling short, she came up with the idea of appealing to the many American fans of her books.

Earlier in the decade Beatrix had been visited by Anne Carroll Moore, Superintendent of Children's Work for the New York Public Library, and through her had welcomed and begun to correspond with a number of other American visitors, many of them librarians or otherwise working in the field. One new colleague was Bertha Mahony, editor of *The Horn Book*, a Boston-based magazine dedicated to children's reading, and it was through her bookshop that Beatrix launched her appeal.

'Peter Rabbit is not begging for himself – and he offers something . . . So many nice kind Americans come through the Lake District on their tour, some of them ask after Peter Rabbit. Do you think any of them would give a guinea (our £1.1.0) to help this fund, in return for an autographed drawing?' Many did, and the experience put her in ever closer touch with an American readership she was inclined to find more sympathetic than the native one. Writers 'take more pains with juvenile literature in America', she would claim in the years ahead – 'children's literature has not been taken seriously over here'.

New Englanders 'appreciate the memories of old times, the simple country pleasures – the lonely hills – and – blessed folk – you are not afraid of being laughed at for sentimental,' she wrote that year, 1927, explaining why she was contemplating another book. It would be longer – a 'proper book' at last – but it would be published only for the American market. *The Fairy Caravan* was something she herself saw as 'too personal – too autobiographical'. 'I rather shrink from submitting the talkings to be pulled about by a matter of fact English publisher, or obtruded on my notice in the *London Daily* …'

> As I walk'd by myself,
> And talked to myself,
> Myself said unto me –

she wrote in the Preface, adding: 'Through many changing seasons these tales have walked and talked with me. They were not meant for printing; I have left them in the homely idiom of our old north country speech.' Indeed, her very useful glossary explained that 'wilf' was the old name for willow, and 'snigging' was dragging a log along the ground with a horse and chain. 'I send them on the insistence of friends beyond the sea.'

Tuppenny the guinea pig, 'rather like a rat without a tail … a very talkative friendly person', would be the hero of *The Fairy Caravan* (1929), the story of a guinea pig who joins a travelling circus.

One of those friends – she would write to him of 'Our Book' – was Henry P. Coolidge, who as a 13 year old had visited Hill Top with his Bostonian mother in the summer of 1927. She wrote admiringly of his lint-white hair; he wrote many years later that she had 'the familiar air of a shrewd, battered, independent Maine fisherman's wife'. Though not very aware of clothes, even I was conscious that she was dowdy.' Beatrix had confided to the Coolidges that her old guinea pig Tuppenny had recently died ('rather like a rat without a tail' she had described him once, 'a very talkative friendly person – only he won't let me touch him'), and on their way back to the States, they sent her two replacements from the pet department of Harrods. A guinea pig called Tuppenny was now to be the central character of *The Fairy Caravan* – a guinea pig whose once sparse hair, anointed with a patent nostrum, just keeps on growing until, to escape teasing, he runs away to join a circus run by Sandy the Highland terrier and Pony Billy.

The Fairy Caravan was Beatrix's most personal book. She especially valued the praise it received from the countrymen around her.

The Fairy Caravan was pieced together from a collection of old stories but its genesis was many-fold. As a girl, Beatrix had repeatedly written about the pleasures of the circus, once noting a menagerie which came to Birnam that featured a man whose beard grew six yards long. (Is it fanciful to remember also the luxuriant locks Beatrix had had before her illness?) Tuppenny, of course, takes his name from her own guinea pig, his twittering speech perfectly recalling the twittering bird-like calls she had noted; she had thought of doing a book about him for Warnes a few years earlier but had been put off by their determination to go only for what would appeal to 'travellers and shops'.

The circus denizens include the dormouse Xarifa – 'a most sweet person, but slumbrous' – named after a beloved dormouse Beatrix had owned. Indeed, echoes of Beatrix's real world are all over the book. The market town where Sandy buys Tuppenny's costume had 'funny crooked streets and little old squares hidden away round corners', and 'archways opening under houses, leading from square to square', just like Hawkshead's own, and 'Mistress Heelis' is mentioned several times.

As the Fairy Caravan wends its slow way through the springtime Lake District landscape, the animals of the circus and those they meet take turns to tell each other stories. The stories dearest to Beatrix's heart are from the chapter called 'The Sheep'. 'That chapter made my old shepherd cry with pleasure; that is appreciation worth having,' she wrote after the book came out, and she had ordered just enough copies privately printed in England to distribute among her friends. She hoped the book would please 'my most exacting critics – my own shepherds and blacksmith. I do not care tuppence about anybody else's opinion.'

'I am conceited enough to say I am the only person who could have written about the sheep; because I know them and the fell like a shepherd.' Mistress Heelis's sheep – Belle Lingcropper, Ruth Twinter, Tibbie Woolstockit – tell of being trapped for thirty days on a high rock ledge, of being buried three weeks 'warm and stuffy' under the snow, and of lambs swept away by flood waters full of snow-broth, having to be rescued by shepherds or sheepdogs ('Sometimes over rough; but faithful'). These were given the names of her own dogs: Kep, Fly and Glen. 'I am afraid I am longwinded about my sheep,' Beatrix confessed.

Opinion over the years has not been kind to this book so close to Beatrix Potter's heart, but she was sufficiently encouraged by its reception to use the same pattern, of publication only in the States, for two later pieces. (These were *Sister Anne*, a bizarre retelling of the Bluebeard story illustrated by another artist, and *Wag-by-Wall*, the country story of an old widow magically rescued from the poorhouse – just as, many years before, *The Tailor of Gloucester* had been.) But that did not mean she had been won wholly back to the publishing world.

'You must remember that I am not a prolific scribbler. I wrote myself out on the rabbit series,' she told her new American publisher. When Warnes persuaded her to produce a year-book, *Peter Rabbit's Almanac*, for 1929, she was adamant the experience was not one she wanted to repeat. The sudden death of Fruing Warne, before the *Almanac* came out, further weakened her emotional bond to the company.

'I never really wanted to print at all,' she wrote after *The Fairy Caravan* appeared, 'but the money has been useful.' She would produce one more 'little book' for 1930 – *The Tale of Little Pig Robinson*, which had begun all those years ago at Sidmouth, when she described the pig on board the ship. But even this tale – longer and more fantastical than usual, with its echoes of Robinson Crusoe and Robert Louis Stevenson's *Kidnapped*, and even of 'The Owl and the Pussycat' – was a slight departure from the books that had made her famous. All the same, the money was useful – not only because of the agricultural depression, but because of Beatrix's growing desire to preserve areas of the Lake District for the National Trust.

In *The Fairy Caravan* Pony Billy ventures into a magic wood to rescue Paddy Pig. If you look closely you can see the fairies among the bluebells.

Trust: 'a quixotic venture'

The end of 1929 saw Beatrix Potter making a vitally important contribution not only to her own property portfolio, but to the lasting beauty of the Lakes. It was not simply her own idea to purchase the 'lovely stretch of mountain and valley' she went to view at Coniston in October. Her Crompton great grandfather had had land there, and she had always longed to buy it back and donate it to the National Trust. If she could do so with the proceeds of *The Fairy Caravan* that would itself be 'like a fairy tale'. It had been in the first instance the National Trust who wanted to buy the Monk Coniston estate, to preserve the land from the hovering developers. As a private individual, however, Beatrix could move more swiftly than they.

But this was a huge purchase – 'an enormous scattered piece', as Beatrix put it in dismay – almost 4000 acres of farms, quarries, woodlands and fells, likely to fetch between £15,000 and £18,000. Notably, it included the lake of Tarn Hows, one of the

Tarn Hows was part of the Monk Coniston estate which Beatrix helped the National Trust to purchase and which she ran for them.

most iconic names in the roll call of Lake District scenery. 'Tarn Hows is too theatrical for my own taste; like scene painting,' Beatrix wrote to Hamer. 'But it appeals to the public, to judge by the numbers yesterday.'

This was too large a prospect for Beatrix to contemplate alone – even had she not been so much more committed to Troutbeck with its 'colly dogs and the galloways and the sheep' than she would ever be to Coniston. The unofficial arrangement between the Heelises and Samuel Hamer was that Beatrix (through William's aegis) would purchase the whole, and that the Trust should then launch an appeal for the money with which to buy back half from her.

The negotiations were tricky, with the owner determined to keep his rights to fish in Tarn Hows. 'We may all end in lunatic asylums', Beatrix warned Hamer towards the end of October. Beatrix's autumn was subsumed into endless visits to see the different parcels of land – to decide which to keep and how to tenant them, to assess the state of timber forests and quarries. But in January 1930 the estate was hers.

The following month John Bailey, Chairman of the National Trust, launched the appeal with a letter to *The Times*, which praised the 'generous and public spirited action of Mrs Heelis'. Beatrix wrote thanking him on 15 February: 'It seems that we have done a big thing; without premeditation; suddenly; inevitably – what else could one do?' Later she would tell Hamer that she was glad she 'had the pluck' not to miss the opportunity. It had been a 'quixotic venture' but it paid off, with continued help from Beatrix and William, who lobbied every wealthy person they knew. By the autumn money had been raised to pay for Tarn Hows and Holme Fell, and Beatrix had decided to donate now, instead of at her death, her great grandfather's Holme Ground. She was immensely touched, however, to find that the National Trust asked her to go on managing the entire Monk Coniston estate on their behalf, not just her own portion.

She took the job so seriously as to be hands-on with every detail. In the first year of her responsibility, letters are full of the 'promiscuous choosing of sites by campers'; the best wording of noticeboards and the best rate for insurance; how she is 'rather unhappy about the Coniston acc[ount]s.' About the sanitation at the Trust's cottages – fifteen people using one earth closet – and about the 'miles & miles of straggling woods … floods, roads, drains and fence renewals'. Three years later she would still

Beatrix took pains also to preserve Yew Tree Farm, another part of the Monk Coniston estate. 'I think the little white farm houses and green fields in the dales are part of the character of the Lake District.'

be writing about litter at Tarn Hows; about whether the one-way traffic rule was not 'rather cruel to nervous drivers'; and how strictly the no-bathing regulation should be enforced. Now in her mid-sixties, however, she was beginning to find that the endless stream of worries, small and large, took a toll.

Beatrix was increasingly aware of mortality. Just before Christmas 1932, the death of her mother left Beatrix a rich woman – but it was a milestone passed, a lost 'link with times that are passed away', leaving Beatrix, at 66, very definitely the older generation at last. As she wrote to her cousin Caroline: 'I am still stiff, always over busy, & feeling old.'

Time, she told Bertha Mahony at the end of 1934, 'slips away faster and faster as one grows older . . . I am "written out" for story books, and my eyes are tired for painting; but I can still take great and useful pleasure in old oak – and drains – and old roofs

– and damp walls – oh the repairs!' She was busy with the restoration of Yew Tree farmhouse, part of the Coniston estate. The 'little white farm houses and green fields' were to her as important an aspect of the Lakes as the dramatic beauty of Tarn Hows.

'I consider Yew Tree is a typical north country farm-house, very well worth preserving' – and so it was, with the spinning gallery running along the barn. She was, she wrote to Hamer, 'totally unrepentant' about the cost of the careful restoration; but to offset some of the costs she decided its parlour should open as a tearoom. Tourists and teas as an alternative source of rural income was another way in which Beatrix was ahead of her time. But her goal was educational as well as financial. Installing some of the old oak furniture she collected at local sales, she wrote at length to Bertha on her beliefs about this then-unfashionable furniture. 'I have always wanted to write a paper on cupboards for the Westmorland & Cumbrian Archeological Society. But I am afraid it is one of the things I shall never do … '

It seemed to be 'more and more of a struggle' to get the day's work done, she told new friends Delmar Banner, a German artist who had moved to the Lake District, and his wife Josefina de Vasconcellos in the autumn of 1936. All the same, as she wrote the following spring to Caroline, there were only one or two things she minded about this business of growing old. '"Thank God I have the seeing eye", that is to say, as I lie in bed I cannot [sic] walk step by step on the fells and rough lands seeing every stone and flower and patch of bog and cotton grass where my old legs will never take me again. Also do you not feel it is rather pleasing to be so much wiser than quantities of young idiots? … I begin to assert myself at 70.'

Endings: 'very far through'

In many ways Beatrix had now reached an equilibrium. She ensconced herself with William in a contented muddle of papers and books, illuminated only by a soft old-fashioned gas or candlelight. (She refused to have electricity in the house, though she agreed it might be installed in the cattle shed – 'the cows may like it'.) Being driven out in an old car known as Noah's Ark with leaks in the roof stopped by an opened umbrella and (so her young relatives remembered) occasionally a sick sheep in the back. She was less concerned with appearances than ever, and used to tell the story of meeting with a tramp one rainy day. 'It's gey weather for the likes of thee and me, missus', he said, looking at the sack draped over her shoulders and taking her for one of his own kind.

The flood of American visitors had slowed, but she had taken to Pekinese dogs – 'very like a guinea pig or a Teddy bear with a tail' – and these were 'good company, but sad pickles,' she wrote, 'always hunting.' There were, however, clouds on the horizon; and not only in the form of the snowclouds which made the winter of 1937/8 a particularly harsh one, with the heaviest fall of snow for 20 years, or because of the outbreak of foot and mouth which followed.

Beatrix was still agitated whenever she saw what she perceived as an error on the part of the National Trust, sending a stream of irate letters about everything from the rights and wrongs of a particular piece of coppicing to the correct type of wire netting for use on the properties she had helped to purchase, but which she was no longer able entirely to control.

In the late 1930s Beatrix purchased further properties in Eskdale and Little Langdale, with the goal of preserving them from development, but intending to manage them herself. She and William had now, however, retired from active management of the Trust's part of the Monk Coniston estate.

The vehemence with which she wrote sheds a revealing light on Beatrix's nature as she aged: for their part, the Trust were always placatory in their reaction – anxious, as

Beatrix at Hill Top in 1939. Hill Top's garden, and another of its gates, would feature in *The Tale of Tom Kitten* (1907).

their representative Bruce Thompson put it, 'to do everything to please Mrs Heelis'. And Beatrix too, in her calmer moments, acknowledged the importance of what they had achieved together. The irritations, she had written earlier, signing off one letter, were after all 'raindrops on the sand. The Trust is a noble thing and – humanly speaking – immortal.

There are some silly mortals connected with it; but they will pass.'

Ulla Hyde Parker, seeing Beatrix and William Heelis in these years, saw them as 'certainly a happy or, perhaps better, a contented couple. They lived harmoniously alongside each other … I remember thinking that they were like two horses in front of the same plough, they walked so steadily beside each other, leaving their furrow behind them.' They were still a very active pair – letters to Josefina de Vasconcellos at the beginning of 1938 describe trips over the fells ('never twice alike'), and note that she and William had missed the aurora because 'W & I were in the cellar with a candle salting 2 pigs legs'. But Beatrix's health was already beginning to be a cause for concern.

In November 1938 she was admitted to the Women's Hospital in Liverpool with 'an insignificant carbuncle'; but the treatment did not end her gynaecological problems. The following March she was back, awaiting a hysterectomy and clearly – from the letter she wrote to Daisy Hammond and Cecily Mills, the young women who had moved to Near Sawrey to help her with the garden – braced for the worst.

'I have failed in strength more than people know these last 2 years. Most times it has been an effort to walk to Hill Top. I am so glad I was feeling particularly well last week; and I have seen the snowdrops again. If it was not for poor WH I would be indifferent to the result. It is such a wonderfully easy going under; and in some ways preferable to a long invalidism, with only old age to follow. Moreover, the whole world seems to be rushing to Armageddon. But not even Hitler can damage the fells.'

If, she continued, 'I do not return Wm will have a list of things I want eventually to go to Hill Top after his death.' Some of her clothes were to go to charity, some to the Manchester museum – 'an Indian shawl that belonged to my grt gr.mother Mrs Ashton of Flowery Field; some muslins and green-silk-high-waist and purple cloak & bonnet of Grandma Leech and a lot of Brussels lace'.

'I hope that Cecily and Wm will walk our little dogs on Sundays; they are old enough to face comment! Could she learn picquet or could you play 3 handed whist? It would be far best for the poor man to follow Willy Gaddum's (her cousin's) example and remarry, provided he did not make a fool of himself by marrying, or not marrying, a servant … I hope and feel sure you will do your best for him in the winter evenings. I have very great confidence in the good sense and kindness of both of you. If I did a kindness in providing a nice house – a lovely house – you provided me with my delightful neighbours.'

To an American friend she wrote that the surgeon 'is somewhat serious. I don't suppose it will be anything worse than "curetting", but anything in the womb is apt to be the beginning of the end. I am in no pain or discomfort, but awfully worried about my husband. You might have noticed I am the stronger minded of the pair, also the money is mine … I have felt very tired and aged these last two years. Maybe the surgeon will put me right – but he cannot put me young again.'

March 31. 39   In hospital Liverpool

Dear Sir,

In case my husband Wm Heelis is too upset not to remember to write, I beg to give formal notice to give up my tenancy of Tilberthwaite farm Coniston in the spring of 1940 but I make the request that you will not announce this publicly or alter the form for a time till we see whether I survive a somewhat serious operation. If I don't you will of course hear & I think my husband would recommend one of my men as tenant. Please keep this quiet in the mean time — I give the notice as a precaution as my executors might be underreasoned; sheep farming is so bad. If & when I retire the Trust should purchase a sufficient landlords stock of sheep — it would be wicked to let them be dispersed a second time after the labour and profitless expense incurred by the shepherd and me, in founding a new heafed flock. Yours truly Beatrix Heelis

to the Secretary
National Trust London

Beatrix's letter from hospital to the National Trust displays a characteristic fortitude and practicality – and a concern not only for her husband, but for her beloved Herdwick sheep.

Beatrix's farewell letters show her at her best – but in this case, they proved premature, though not without some problems on the way. In early April she was writing to Daisy Hammond from hospital: 'No one can be more surprised to be writing to you again. I do not think it is merciful to put an old woman through such an experience. I was sick again on Sunday, and burst the stitches, so had a third journey "downstairs" to be sewn up again … '

In May she was 'said to be completely cured' though she still walked with a stick. Two months later she was rushed back to hospital again with what was said to be appendicitis, but a letter from hospital to Daisy Hammond was concerned with making blackcurrant jelly, and the correct feeding of calves. 'I feel remarkably well.' But 1939, of course, was providing other challenges.

The hills and fields around Hill Top are where Beatrix asked that her ashes should be scattered. The Lakeland scenery gave Beatrix consolation even in the dark days of war. 'Hitler cannot spoil the fells; the rocks and fern and lakes and waterfalls will outlast us all.'

The year before, Beatrix had described Hitler as 'a brutal raving lunatic … the ranting note and the smiling face in the telegraphed photographs are not sane'. Then, she could 'think of nothing but forebodings'. But in the event, daily life went on despite the outbreak of war.

Though the shipyards of Barrow were only 15 miles from the Lakes, she and farmers like her found the first real danger was the deluge of government forms and regulations. Beatrix was able to congratulate herself that both she and William were engaged on 'useful work, but not hard work this time' – unlike the previous war. The following spring ('rather crippled, though still smiling and very busy') she was writing happily about the sheets of bluebells, and of how the 'hawthorn hedges and big thorn bushes in the valleys have been like snow drifts'.

These were, however, the days when England feared the worst. On 5 June, the day after Dunkirk – 'No one can foretell the end … We must do our bit, and the colonies will carry on the cause of freedom if we go under … If things get worse I think I'll bury some tins of biscuits in the woods!' Even the original *Peter Rabbit* drawings had been sent back to her for safekeeping, out of London and away from the bombs; the Hyde Parker family had taken refuge with her when Ulla's husband Willie was injured in the blackout and Melford Hall commandeered by the army.

News of the destruction of her 'unloved birthplace' in Bolton Gardens left her unmoved.

But as the war wore on – with the air raids on the north in late 1941, with the advent of food shortages – it took a heavy toll. Beatrix found relief for her feelings in writing letters to friends, though she didn't post all of them. More men were called up. Beatrix had, moreover continued trouble with the wound from her operation which had left her 'badly ruptured' – forced to support her stomach with a band of elastic, and elastic was now hard to find.

But she was still alive to the possibilities of her work, sending stories she envisaged using in a sequel to *The Fairy Caravan* away to America for safe-keeping. She was gratified, in the spring of 1942, to receive a 'prodigious' royalty cheque – her books, with their tales of deadly peril escaped, seemed more popular than ever in these dangerous times.

The winter of 1942/3 saw her busy as the drive to produce food, and wool, for a beleaguered nation placed farmers under ever more pressure. In March Beatrix was voted in as the next president, for 1944, of the Herdwick Sheep-Breeders' Association. She would have been the first woman to hold the position – had she lived to occupy it.

In the early months of 1943 Beatrix was still cheerful. It was now that she sent to Josefina de Vasconcellos a letter with a sketch of herself as Mrs Tiggy-winkle; her own solid figure and customary suit below a twinkling hedgehog's face. 'HBH a portrait', it is labelled – Helen Beatrix Heelis – and 'motto Keep Smiling!'

Earlier in the letter she had written: 'I think in difficult times the true philosophy is to keep the mind so far as possible to the trivial round and common task, thinking as little as may be about the things which we cannot mend.' Years before, writing to Norman Warne about *The Tale of Mrs Tiggy-Winkle*, she had jokingly compared the washerwoman to Lady Macbeth, and strange though the comparison may seem, perhaps Lady Macbeth's determination to brush on through – her insistence that 'a little water clears us of this deed' – did have an echo in the hedgehog laundrywoman, and in Beatrix herself too.

She could enjoy the spring, and the gaiety of the June garden – 'white bell flowers everywhere among the weeds, and the house covered with roses', and continue her work of the last few years, arranging Hill Top for posterity. She could still be touched by tributes like those of the Guides who still camped on her land, and who now decided each to dress up as one of her characters to celebrate her birthday. But in September she took to her bed with a bronchial cough which strained a heart long weakened by her youthful rheumatic fever. 'I don't think much about it, and I was often worse in London. But if an old person of 77 continues to play these games – well it can be done once too often.'

In early November she had 'not quite got rid of the doctor, but I hope if the weather improves I may get back to my usual health – or nearly so – one must expect to lose a little ground as one gets older.' It was not to be.

On 13 December she wrote to her shepherd Joe Moscrop, in pencil and an unsteady hand: 'Very far through, but still some kick in me. Am not going right way at present. I write a line to shake you by the hand, our friendship has been entirely pleasant. I am very ill with bronchitis.' On the night of 22 December Beatrix Potter died, with William by her side.

On the evening of her death she sent for Tom Storey, and gave him instructions as to where she wanted her ashes to be scattered. 'I want it kept a secret.' Tom may later have confided the secret to his son Geoff before his death in 1986, but since Geoff himself died some years later, her resting place is as private as she wished. One may stand today in the porch at Hill Top and gaze up at the swell of hills above, and to the line of trees against which Jemima Puddle-duck finally took flight – but Beatrix Potter's ashes are long absorbed into this beloved corner of her Lancashire Lakes.

Jemima Puddle-duck and Mrs Tiggy-winkle

Jemima Puddle-duck confides to the 'sandy whiskered gentleman'
her desire to find somewhere safe to lay her eggs.

A few years before her death, showing her portfolios in 1940 to a young New Zealand admirer, Beatrix stopped at the picture of Jemima Puddle-duck rushing down the hill and said to him: 'that is what I used to look like to the Sawrey people. I rushed about quacking industriously!'

The 1908 *Tale of Jemima Puddle-Duck* (and the 1925 *Painting Book* which followed) describes the misadventures of a white Aylesbury duck, distraught because her eggs are regularly taken away and given to hens to sit on. Beatrix surely got the idea from observing the practice of Mrs Cannon, the wife of the Hill Top farmer, who herself appears with her children Betsy and Ralph, to whom the book is dedicated.

Determined to find a place where she can hatch her eggs herself, Jemima leaves the farm and encounters in the woods a 'sandy whiskered gentleman' who politely invites her to lay them in his shed – a shed most curiously full of feathers. Hill Top Farm, like many others, lost a lot of barnyard fowl to the fox.

Jemima, however has no suspicions; and despite her folly there is a frisson of sheer horror when the fox sends her off, all unwitting, to pick the sage, parsley and onions with which she is herself to be stuffed for his dinner. It is a retelling of Little Red Riding Hood – but Beatrix often used the theme of predator and prey, while gentlemen of suave appearance and polished manners, ready to prey on any foolish female, are of course the subject of many a human story.

The portrait of Beatrix by her friend, the artist Delmar Banner, now hangs in the National Portrait Gallery.

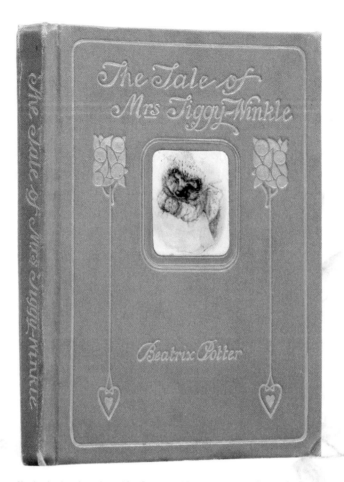

The hedgehog laundress Mrs Tiggy-winkle was based on Beatrix's own pet hedgehog Mrs Tiggy, who 'used to lay her prickles flat back to be stroked'.

Jemima is rescued by the sagacious farm collie Kep (named for Beatrix's own favourite collie), with the help of two hound puppies – which, however, gobble up her eggs. Soon after she lays more eggs and is at last allowed to keep them herself. Only four hatch, however – 'Jemima Puddle-duck said that it was because of her nerves; but she had always been a bad sitter,' writes Beatrix coolly. The character – perhaps Beatrix's best-known, after Peter Rabbit – was probably named for the Jemima Blackburn who wrote the book on birds Beatrix had been given as a child, and of whose lack of sentimentality she had spoken admiringly. As so often, the book draws on recognisable locations from Sawrey – the gate to the vegetable garden at Hill Top, the village pub called The Tower Bank Arms. And, perhaps most personally of all, the hills above Sawrey where Jemima achieves flight are the same surrounding hills where Beatrix asked that her ashes should be scattered.

Though Beatrix compared herself to Jemima Puddle-duck, photographs of her in later life bear a marked resemblance to another of her famous female characters – the hedgehog laundress Mrs Tiggy-winkle, whose *Tale* she had published in 1905. The likeness is clearest in a photograph taken by Delmar Banner, whose subsequent painting is in the National Portrait Gallery. Beatrix herself sketched for Josefina de Vasconcellos, Delmar Banner's wife, a caricature of herself 'like Mrs Tiggy-Winkle'. 'She knew she was like one of her own little animals,' Josefina said.

Mrs Tiggy-winkle's eyes 'went twinkle, twinkle', her stocky figure was slightly hunched. Mrs Tiggy-winkle was, moreover, as meticulous a craftswoman as Beatrix herself, 'exorcising', in Beatrix's word, spots and stains. The character was based on Kitty MacDonald, a Scottish washerwoman the Potter family had employed over the years at Dalguise, and about whom Beatrix wrote repeatedly. 'Kitty is eighty-three', she told her diary then, 'but waken, and delightfully merry … a comical, round little old woman, as brown as a berry and wears a multitude of petticoats and a white mutch' – just as Beatrice herself would wear a linen cap.

Left Kep the collie recruits two hound pups to help him rescue Jemima. As so often, Beatrix used a familiar building for her illustration.
Right The Tower Bank Arms, pictured in *The Tale of Jemima Puddle-Duck* (1908).

Mrs Tiggy-winkle and Lucie return the laundry to Peter Rabbit and Benjamin Bunny.

The character also comes, of course, from one of Beatrix's own pet hedgehogs, Mrs Tiggy. In 1904, when she was doing the drawings for the book, 'Mrs Tiggy as a model is comical', Beatrix wrote – 'so long as she can go to sleep on my knee she is delighted, but if she is propped up on end for half an hour, she first begins to yawn pathetically, and then she does bite! Never the less she is a dear person; just like a very fat, rather stupid little dog.' Many years later, long after Mrs Tiggy's death, Beatrix still remembered how she used to lay her prickles flat back to be stroked. In the book, however, Mrs Tiggy-winkle is a slightly disconcerting creature – 'fairy beasts', Beatrix once called hedgehogs – whose clothes conceal her animal nature from the human child at the centre of the tale.

As Mrs Tiggy-winkle and a little girl called Lucie deliver the clean laundry to the local animals, Peter Rabbit and others make an appearance. But the figure of Lucie – Lucie Carr, one of the daughters of the Newlands vicar who Beatrix met while holidaying at Lingholm – was one of Beatrix's few failures. She knew she could not draw people, she herself said.

All the same, the real Lucie was one of the recipients of the miniature letters Beatrix wrote to children, about various of her characters. The lucky children might receive complaints from Mrs Josephine Rabbit (mother of Peter) about the amount of starch Mrs Tiggy-winkle had used – or Mr Jeremy Fisher's grumble that he had received a large handkerchief instead of a frog-sized tablecloth; 'If this continues every week, Mr. J. Fisher will have to get married, so as to have the washing done at home.'

The hedgehog laundress in *The Tale of Mrs Tiggy-Winkle* (1905) was based on Beatrix's own pet hedgehog – 'a dear person; just like a very fat, rather stupid little dog'.

Afterlife

FABULA DE
PETRO CUNICULO

BEATRICIS POTTER

F. WARNE & CO LTD

Beatrix Potter's works have even been translated
include Latin, braille and hieroglyphics.

In every possible sense of the word, Beatrix Potter left a considerable legacy. The first to feel it – to shoulder what he found a considerable burden – was of course William; trying to ensure that her farms continued to be managed as she would wish. 'I am trying to carry on all the farm as usual', William wrote to Joe Moscrop some six weeks later, 'but I feel lost without the "Head".'

Beatrix's estate was considerable – more than £200,000, perhaps seven million in today's money. Hill Top was indeed to be preserved as she decreed, as a 'permanent "memorial"'; first opened to the public on July 8 1946, admission 1 shilling. Her original drawings, rescued from behind the geyser at Castle Cottage, were taken there to be displayed for forty years, until being removed first for conservation, and then to go to the new Beatrix Potter Gallery in Hawkshead, created from what had once been William's law office. (The original illustrations of *The Tailor of Gloucester* would go eventually to the Tate Gallery, and those of *The Tale of the Flopsy Bunnies* to the British Museum.)

Beatrix's portfolios of botanical drawings, on her wishes, went to the Armitt Library in Ambleside, where they remain today, along with her archeological drawings. In 1997 the Linnean Society publicly acknowledged that she had been 'treated scurvily' a hundred years before. The theories she developed for herself are generally accepted today. A scientist visiting Hill Top told staff that he still used her drawings in demonstrations for his students, and in 1967 W.P.K. Findlay, himself a former president of the British Mycological Society, used them to illustrate his *Wayside and Woodland Fungi*. Beatrix once wrote to her cousin's five-year-old son: 'I have been drawing funguses very hard, I think some day they will be put in a book but it will be a dull one to read.' Well, this would be dull to a five year old, probably.

William was to enjoy the rights and revenues of Beatrix's books for his lifetime – but William proved to survive her by only eighteen months, his ashes scattered on the same spot as hers, on the hills above Sawrey. They passed then to Norman Warne's nephew Frederick; and thence to the Frederick Warne company (who also hold the original drawings for *The Tale of Peter Rabbit*). It is they who are still responsible for her literary legacy.

Over 150 million Beatrix Potter books have been sold over the years. They have been translated into more than 35 languages including Latin and Lowland Scots, to say nothing of hieroglyphics. More recently Peter Rabbit has become the mascot of Mitsubishi (Beatrix Potter is hugely popular in Japan, where a theme park boasts a perfect replica of Hill Top Farm.) The Peter Rabbit marketing operations boasts 200 licensees worldwide, in more than 110 countries. Besides the tv adaptations of the stories – *The World of Peter Rabbit* and Friends in the early Nineties, and the 2012 CGI-animated CBeebies series *Peter Rabbit* – as the 150th anniversary of her birth approaches, a new live action/animated hybrid film is said to be on the way.

1971 saw the film *The Tales of Beatrix Potter*, mounted by the Royal Ballet and choreographed by Frederick Ashton (who himself danced the role of Mrs Tiggy-winkle), with Wayne Sleep as Squirrel Nutkin and Tom Thumb. In 1992 came a stage version, adapted by Anthony Dowell, whose critical reception did not prevent it's being several times revived in recent years – or prevent audiences enjoying it. In 1996 Patricia Routledge took the title role in *Beatrix*, a stage play based on Beatrix Potter's life by Patrick Garland and Potter expert Judy Taylor which opened at the Chichester Festival Theatre.

More recently, of course, audiences have come to Beatrix through *Miss Potter*, with Renée Zellweger in the title role. The idea was mooted in 1992, more than a decade before the film was made, when lyricist and Broadway director Richard Maltby, Jr was holidaying in the Blue Ridge Mountains in Virginia and, looking for something to read to his young children, found a book of Beatrix Potter stories on the hotel bookshelf. The script he wrote was loved by everybody to whom he showed it. But it was not actually sold to anybody until it came to the attention of a new set of producers in 2003, with Cate Blanchett lined up to play Beatrix.

They formed the appropriately named Hopping Mad Productions, but before shooting started Cate Blanchett had dropped out, and Renee Zellweger and director Chris Noonan, of *Babe*, came in. Filming began March 7 2006 in London and the Isle of Man, where the interiors for the Potter family home and for Hill Top were created. The principal exterior scenes were shot in the Lakes, but even then the more open Yew Tree stood in for Hill Top. The film paints a Beatrix Potter Chris Noonan saw as 'a standard-bearer for women's rights, without putting those things into strong language' – a woman who had 'to fight for the right to have her stories published – and to marry when she wanted'.

It's true that while Beatrix was no supporter of the suffrage movement – while she hailed a happy marriage as the crown of a woman's life – she spent much of her life pushing the boundaries of what might have been expected from a woman of her class and her time. But perhaps it is also true that everyone makes a Potter for their own day.

What we want today is a complex heroine, and here Beatrix Potter's diaries are the key. They were revealed to us by an unlikely champion – Leslie Linder, an engineer specialising in lifting tackle, who in 1945 found himself in charge of the children's library at his local Congregational Church. He thought of Beatrix Potter's work, which he had himself enjoyed as a child, and to find out more about the author soon became a consuming hobby.

Beginning the collection of photographs and of Beatrix's artwork – more than 2000 items in all – which would eventually be left to the Victoria and Albert Museum, he also began taking his holidays in the Lake District. There, no-one had yet deciphered the many pages of cipher writing which even Beatrix herself claimed not to be able to read in her latter days.

For several years Linder puzzled away at what turned out to be a highly individual alphabet code – only to crack it on Easter Monday 1958, just as he was about to give up the attempt. Translating the whole 200,000 words took another five years, and

THE JOURNAL OF
BEATRIX POTTER
❦ *from 1881 to 1897* ❦

Transcribed from her code writings by LESLIE LINDER

Left The 2006 feature film *Miss Potter* cast Renee Zellweger as Beatrix, with Ewan McGregor as
Norman Warne and Emily Watson as his sister Millie.
Right A translation of Beatrix's coded diaries was finally published in 1966, a century after her birth.

publication was delayed yet further by qualms the Executors of the Heelis Estate
felt over some of the passages. Nonetheless the diary came out in July 1966, for the
centenary of Beatrix's birth, with some pages about Beatrix's family, or about religious
affairs, deleted. These were reinstated for a new edition in 1989. What the diaries show
is a Beatrix who fits into the line of great Victorian women – Florence Nightingale,
Elizabeth Barrett Browning – who won through to personal freedom and valuable
work late and only with great pain. Darkness alternating with humour, they also show
an artist who very consciously created and judged herself as writer and illustrator.

Names like Peter Rabbit and Squirrel Nutkin have become part of the English
language – just as 'Romeo and Juliet' are words familiar even to those who have not
read Shakespeare, or a Dalek conjures up an image whether or not you've watched *Dr
Who*. 1980 saw the foundation of the Beatrix Potter Society 'to promote the study and
appreciation of the life and works of Beatrix Potter'.

She herself said that: 'I have just made stories to please myself, because I never grew
up'. But others have been trying to assess her work since her own day. In February
1943 she wrote scathingly to the author of a *Listener* article comparing her to Blake,
Constable, Bewick, Caldecott – 'the Immortals,' as Beatrix put it. 'I think I have "done

my bit"; – unconsciously – trying to copy nature – without affectation or swelled head.' But the article, she declared, was 'surely great rubbish? Absolute bosh.' Ten years before her death, no less a person than Graham Greene, writing in the *London Mercury*, had been given similarly short shrift. He had described her 'selective realism, which takes emotion for granted and puts aside love and death with gentle detachment'. The comment is perceptive. But Greene went further declaring that on the evidence of characters like Mr Tod, Beatrix Potter must, between 1907 and 1909, 'have passed through an emotional ordeal which changed the character of her genius'. Beatrix hastened to inform him that she had merely been suffering from the flu.

But she herself said that 'there is more in the books than mere funniness'. Her friend Delmar Banner claimed that her unsentimental portrayal of relationships was one that would help children later in life. Others have noted the internal rigour of the world she creates – the ways that, as Ewan McGregor, who played Norman Warne in *Miss Potter*, put it: 'They are still animals even if they're wearing coats.'

A recent exhibition in the British Library, *Animal Tales*, featured a selection of authors from Aesop to Ted Hughes, and works from *Black Beauty* to *Old Possum's Book of Practical Cats*. Beatrix Potter was placed alongside the pioneering naturalist Gilbert White, in the category of those whose achievement lies in encouraging us actually to look at animals.

The exhibition explored the way in which, while the Victorians saw an affinity between childhood innocence and a sentimentalised view of animals, 'after Darwin and Freud, neat distinctions between humans and animals blurred, as writers began to explores the instincts that lie only partly hidden beneath our civilized veneer.' At a very young age, Beatrix Potter explicitly rejected sentimentality, and at some point in each story her animals tend to lose their human clothes. (It is only after he sheds his jacket and takes to all four feet, instead of walking man-like on two, that Peter Rabbit finally escapes from Mr McGregor.) She was working after Darwin but before most of Freud's publications – but in this, as in a good deal else, Beatrix Potter was ahead of her time.

One aspect of Beatrix Potter's legacy, however, stands largely apart from the changes of the years. 'Hitler cannot spoil the fells; the rocks and fern and lakes and waterfalls will outlast us all,' Beatrix said in the foreshadow of war. She took steps to ensure that the mixed blessings of peace and progress should likewise leave them intact.

Two months after Beatrix's death, the National Trust announced 'Greatest Ever Lakeland Gift'. It was an indeed an extraordinary package Beatrix had left them (and legacies from William himself would swell it yet further) – more than 4000 acres, fifteen farms, forests and houses – areas which, but for her intervention, would surely have been developed long ago.

'For years I have been gradually picking up land, chance bargains, and specializing on road frontages and the heads of valleys,' she had told a correspondent a few years before. 'I own two or three strikingly beautiful spots. The rest is pleasant peaceful country, foreground of the hills, I think more liable to be spoilt than the high fells themselves.'

When the Lake District National Park was set up in 1951, all her bequest was encompassed within it. That might not have pleased her – she did not quite understand the aim of the plan which had been mooted even in her lifetime but, she told Delmar Banner, 'I am sure it means interference with other people's property.' Inevitably in a changing world – and one that has become even more challenging for farmers – there have had, controversially, to be changes made to the farming practice she envisaged. But as her will decreed, it is the grey Herdwick sheep which still roam her hills.

She described those hills in an essay for *The Horn Book*, eighteen months before her death. In 'The Lonely Fells' she wrote of how, over Troutbeck Tongue, the mist 'takes strange shapes when it rises at sunset. During storms it rushes down the valleys like a black curtain billowing before the wind, while the Troutbeck River thunders over the Cauldron. Memories of "old unhappy far-off things and battles long ago"; sorrows of yesterday and today and tomorrow the vastness of the fells covers all with a mantle of peace.'

When younger and fitter she had loved to wander there, stopping to eat her bread and cheese by a boulder, or under the stone shelter the shepherds used. Sometimes with a sheepdog, Nip or Fly – 'more often I went alone. But never lonely. There was company of gentle sheep, and wild flowers and singing waters. I listened to the voices of the Little Folk.' 150 years after her birth, and in a world she might not always recognize, thanks to the writings of Beatrix Potter, we can listen to those voices still.

Discovering More

Hilltop and the Beatrix Potter Gallery.

Lake District

Hill Top and Near Sawrey

Beatrix Potter's beloved home is at once a shrine to her memory, and a house and garden which allows you to believe she might still walk in any day. The village of Near Sawrey is full of sites featured in her books, from the Tower Bank Arms and the Buckle Yeat Guest House, to what was once Ginger and Pickles's shop; as well as Castle Farm where Beatrix and William Heelis lived. From Near Sawrey it is an easy walk down to Esthwaite Water (past the signpost featured in *The Tale of Pigling Bland*), or up to Moss Eccles Tarn.

Beatrix Potter Gallery, Hawkshead

Many of Beatrix's drawings are now housed in the evocative setting of what was once William's law office, where artefacts like the big specimen cabinet she shared with her brother may also be on display. The village of Hawkshead is itself enchanting, full of narrow streets and archways Beatrix drew. William Wordsworth was a pupil at the carefully preserved Grammar School.

Armitt Museum and Library, Ambleside

Both Beatrix and her husband had strong associations with the Armitt Trust Library, to whom she bequeathed her drawings of fungi and many books. The museum, with its atmospheric library, boasts a fascinating exhibition on her life and work. Close by, the Ambleside Bridge House is a 17th-century survival Beatrix was eager to preserve.

Wray Castle, Ambleside

The neo-Gothic house where the Potter family stayed may not boast the furnished interiors of many other National Trust properties, but instead it offers an experience young children will enjoy, as well as the chance to arrive by boat at the Castle's own jetty. Another family favourite is the World of Beatrix Potter Attraction at Bowness-on-Windermere; an interactive exhibition on Beatrix Potter's stories, with an award-winning tea room.

Wray Castle, where Beatrix stayed in 1882.

Catbells towards Skelgill.

Coniston, Troutbeck

The dramatic beauty of Tarn Hows makes it perhaps the best known of the Lake District sites Beatrix helped to preserve. But in fact many of the fells, and the farms, around Coniston to the west of Lake Windermere, and Troutbeck to the east, owe their unspoilt state to Beatrix's care.

Derwentwater and Catbells

Further to the north is another area where Beatrix holidayed in her youth, and which provided the setting for many of her stories. Derwentwater is the site of St Herbert's

Island, as visited by Squirrel Nutkin, while a walk around the western flank of Catbells gives you the settings for *The Tale of Mrs Tiggy-Winkle*.

Southern England

Melford Hall, Long Melford, Suffolk

The turreted sixteenth-century home of Beatrix's Hyde Parker relations – now in the care of the National Trust, but still occupied by the family – boasts a number of Potter works and legacies. A lace shawl she gave to Ulla, her original Jemima Puddle-duck doll, the fireplace she sketched and the bedroom where she stayed. The gardens were a particular source of inspiration.

The House of the Tailor of Gloucester, College Court, Gloucester

A charming old world house in the shadow of the Cathedral, the area Beatrix drew for her favourite book, now hosts a shop and small museum run by volunteers and dedicated to her work and memory.

South Kensington Museums

The extensive Beatrix Potter archive of the Victoria and Albert Museum is held at Blythe House in Olympia, which may be visited by appointment – though items may be on special display also in the main South Kensington buildings. Next door to the V&A, the Natural History Museum still features much that Beatrix would recognise, not least the dramatic Romanesque architecture.

Scotland

Beatrix Potter Exhibition and Garden, Birnam, Dunkeld

The Birnam Arts Centre, in the area where Beatrix spent such memorable holidays, boasts an exhibition and garden celebrating her characters. Dalguise House itself is now a centre for children's adventure holidays.

Selected further reading

A History of the Writings of Beatrix Potter, Leslie Linder (Frederick Warne 1971)

A Victorian Naturalist: Beatrix Potter's Drawings from the Armitt Collection, Anne Stevenson Hobbs, Eileen Jay, Beatrix Potter (Frederick Warne 1992

Beatrix Potter's Letters, selected and introduced by Judy Taylor (Frederick Warne 1989)

Beatrix Potter: The extraordinary life of a Victorian genius, Linda Lear (Allen Lane 2007)

Beatrix Potter: Artist, Storyteller and Countrywoman, Judy Taylor (Frederick Warne 1986/2014)

Cousin Beatie: A Memory of Beatrix Potter, Ulla Hyde Parker (Frederick Warne 1981)

Letters to Children, foreword Philip Hofer (Harvard College Library 1966)

She Was Loved: Memories of Beatrix Potter, Josefina de Vasconcellos (Titus Wilson 2003)

That Naughty Rabbit: Beatrix Potter and Peter Rabbit, Judy Taylor (Frederick Warne 1987)

The Journal of Beatrix Potter 1881–1897, transcribed and edited Leslie Linder (Frederick Warne 1989)

The Tale of Beatrix Potter, Margaret Lane (Frederick Warne 1946)

The Magic Years of Beatrix Potter, Margaret Lane (Frederick Warne 1978)

The publications by the Beatrix Potter Society which I found of assistance are too numerous to mention individually. I was also lucky enough also to receive invaluable guidance from (in the Lake District) Liz Hunter MacFarlane and Catherine Pritchard of the National Trust, and Graham Kilner of the Armitt Museum and Library; from Professor R.G. West in Cambridge . . . and from many other among the Beatrix Potter devotees who scatter the globe!

Index

Page numbers in *italic* refer to the illustrations

Aesop *44*
Appley Dapply's Nursery Rhymes 106, 107
Aris, Ernest A. 61
Armitt Library, Ambleside 144, 151
Ashton, Frederick 145
Aunt Pettitoes 98–9
Austen, Jane 79

Bailey, John 127
Banner, Delmar 129, *139*, 141, 148, 149
Bath 79
Beatrix (play) 145
Beatrix Potter Gallery, Hawkshead 144, 151
Beatrix Potter Society 147
Benjamin Bunny *35*, *39*, 40, 42, *43*, 58, 73, *73*
Benson, 'Tant' 118
Birnam, Dunkeld 42, 45, 153
Blackburn, Jemima 27, 140
Blanchett, Cate 146
Bolton Gardens, South Kensington 16–17, *17*, 22, 90, 135
British Library, London 148
British Museum, London 144
Brock the Badger 91

Caldecott, Randolph 21
Calvin, John 20
Cameron, Miss 34
Camfield Place, Essendon, Hertfordshire 19, 22–3
Cannon, John 82, 105
Cannon, Mrs 138

Cannon, Ralph 84, 138
Carr, Lucie 142
Carroll, Lewis *20*, 21
Carter, Annie *see* Moore, Annie
Cartland, Barbara 23
Castle Cottage, Near Sawrey 6, 8, 93, *94–5*, 102, 144
Castle Farm, Sawrey 93
Catbells 152, *152*
Cecily Parsley's Nursery Rhymes 111, *112*, *113*
Chichester Festival Theatre 145
Choyce, Louie 104–5, 113
Cockshott Point 120, *120*
Coniston 126–9, 152
Coolidge, Henry P. 122

Dalguise, Scotland *23*, 24–6, *24*, 30
Derwentwater *70*, 71, 152
Disney, Walt 61
Dowell, Anthony 145
Doyle, Arthur Conan 67

Eskdale 130
Esthwaite Water *54*, 55, 85

The Fairy Caravan 12–13, 121, *121*, 122–4, *122*, *125*, 126, 136
Falmouth 42, 49
The Field 58
Findlay, W.P.K. 145
Flopsy Bunnies 60, 88, 91
Flower, Sir William 52

Garland, Patrick 145
Gaskell, Mrs 22
Gaskell, William 22, 58

Ginger 88–9
Gladstone, W.E. 22
Gloucester *66*, 68, 70–1, 153
Greene, Graham 148
Grimwades *109*, 111
Gwaynynog, Wales 74, 80, 88

Hamer, Samuel 115, 127, 129
Hammond, Daisy 132, 133
Harescombe Grange, Gloucestershire 50, 73
Harrods 72, 122
Hawkshead 119, 123, 144, 151
Heelis, William 6, 98, 113, 149
  marriage to Beatrix 7–8, 93–6, *97*, 98, 100–1, 102, 131
  country dancing 104, *104*
  and Beatrix's ill-health and death 132, 137, 144, 145
Herdwick sheep 112–13, 116, *116–17*, 136, 149
Hildesheimer and Faulkner *39*
Hill, Octavia 113
Hill Top, Near Sawrey 7–13, *9–12*, *134–5*, 136, 137, 150, *150*
  Beatrix buys 80–6
  garden *10*, *14–15*, *80–1*, *85*, *105*, *131*
  as setting for Beatrix's books 7, 85–6, *86*, 139, 140
  after Beatrix's death 144
  Japanese theme park 145
Hitler, Adolf 132, 134, 148
Holme Fell 127
Holme Ground 127
The Horn Book 149
Hunca Munca 73–4, *75*
Hunter, Sir Robert 113
Hutton, Caroline (BP's cousin) 50, 68, 76, 85, 93, 128, 129

Invalid Children's Aid Association 61

Japan 145
Jemima Puddle-Duck 13, *84*, 85, 91, 137, 138–41, *138*
Jeremy Fisher 49, 83–5, *87*, 142
John Dormouse 88

Kep *81*, 85, 140
Keswick 49, 83
Kew Gardens, London 52–4, 55–6

Lake District 30, 55, 57, 126–9, 149, 150–2
Le Fleming, Christopher 61
Lear, Edward 21, *21*
Leech, Grandma 19, 132
Lennel, Scotland 50
Liberty 72
Linder, Leslie 146–7
Lindeth Howe, Windermere 93, 103
Lingholm, Cumbria 57, 83, 142
Linnean Society 56–7, 144
The Listener 147–8
Little Langdale 130
Little Pig Robinson 50
London Mercury 148

MacDonald, Kitty 141
McGregor, Ewan 148
McIntosh, Charlie 47, 49, 56
Mahony, Bertha 120, 128
Maltby, Richard, Jr 145–6
Manchester 19
Massee, George 54–7
Melford Hall, Long Melford, Suffolk *48*, 49, *51*, 85, 135, 153
Middleton family 61
Millais, Effie 22
Millais, John Everett 22, 26, 30

Mills, Cecily 132
Miss Potter (film) 145–6, *147*, 148
Mr Tod 45, *82*, 91, 101, 148
Mrs Tiggy-winkle 13, 74, 78, 79, 88, 136, 141–2, *142–3*, 145
Mitsubishi 145
Monk Coniston 126–9, 130
Moore, Anne Carroll 120
Moore, Annie (née Carter) 34, 38, 42, 57
Moore, Edwin 38
Moore, Eric 49
Moore, Freda 68
Moore, Marjorie 62
Moore, Noel *46*, 49, 58–9, 62
Moore, Norah 71
Morley Memorial College 52
Moscrop, Joe 116–18, 137, 144
Moss Eccles Tarn 102, *103*

National Trust 8–11, 13, 113, 115–16, 120, 124, 126–9, 130–1, 149
Natural History Museum, London 38, 52, 153
Near Sawrey, Cumbria 6–8, 55, 80–3, 88–9, *88*, 101, 102–3, 112, 140, 150
Nister, Ernest 50
Noonan, Chris 146

Old Brown 29, *69*, 71

Parker, Ulla Hyde 6–8, 13, 19, 118, 131, 135
Parker, William Hyde 49
Peter Piper 47–9, *47*, 58–9
Peter Rabbit *46*, 47–9, 58–61, *58–60*, 62, 72, *72*, 73, 88, *109*, *110*, 120, 142, 145, 147, 148
Peter Rabbit series (CBeebies) 145
Peter Rabbit's Almanac 61, 124

Peter Rabbit's Painting Book 60, 91, *92*, 107
Pickles 88–9
The Pie and the Patty-pan 76, 77
Pigling Bland 96, 98–101, *98–101*
Post Office (UK) 61
Postlethwaite, John 86
Potter, Alice Crompton *16*
Potter, Beatrix *6*, *16*, *23*, *27*, *62–3*, *119*
  early life 16–29
  appearance 6, 141
  collections 8–11, *8*, *9*
  diary 13, 30–40, *34*, 56, 78, 146–7, *147*
  love of nature 17, 26–7, 45
  family background 19
  education 20–1, 38
  sketchbooks *25*, 26, *26*, *28*
  pets 27–9, *35*, *36*, 42–5, *43*
  artistic training 30–7
  ill-health 37–8, 93, 131–3, 136–7
  sells drawings *39*, 40–1
  study of fungi 45–7, 49, 50–1, 52–7, *53*, 144–5
  picture letters *46*, 49–50, 57, 58–9, 62, 68, 71, 78–9, 142
  interest in fossils 50–1
  and Norman Warne 71, 74–9, 80, 98, 102
  secondary merchandise 72, *109*, *110*, 111
  political activities 90, 91
  land purchases 93, 102, 113–16, 126–7, 130
  marriage 7–8, 93–6, *97*, 98, 100–1, 102, 131
  as a farmer 103–6, 108, 112–18, *117*, 136
  and problems at Warne's 104, 106–9
  eye problems 107–8, *109*
  and the National Trust 113, 115–16, 120, 124, 126–9, 130–1, 149
  fund-raising in America 120
  in old age 129, 130–7, *133*

death 137
portrait of *139*, 141
legacy 144, 149
see also Hill Top *and individual books*
Potter, Bertram (BP's brother) *11*, 19, *23*, 29, 35, 38, 40, 93, 108
Potter, Edmund (BP's grandfather) 19
Potter, Helen (BP's mother) 19, *23*, 34, 50, 74, 76, 93–6, 103, 128
Potter, Jessie Crompton (BP's grandmother) 19
Potter, Rupert (BP's father) 16, 21, *23*
photographs *16–18*, 22
Unitarianism 17–19
paintings 22
and Beatrix's childhood 22, 24
ill-health 57, 90, 102
and Beatrix's publishing career 67
disapproves of Norman Warne 76
and Beatrix's marriage to William Heelis 93–6
death 102
Pritchard, John 68

Rawnsley, Canon Hardwicke 30, 57, 59, 62–6, *63*, 91, 113
The Roly-Poly Pudding 86
Roscoe, Sir Henry Enfield (BP's uncle) 40, 52–6
Routledge, Patricia 145
Royal Ballet 145
Royal Botanic Gardens (Kew Gardens), London 52–4, 55–6
Royal Mint 61
Ruskin, John 22, 30

St Herbert's Island, Derwentwater *70*, 71
Samuel Whiskers 13, 86, *86*, 101
Sanderson's 72

Sawrey *see* Near Sawrey
Scotland 22, 24–6, 42, 50–1, 153
Scott, Sir Walter 21
Sister Anne 124
Sleep, Wayne 145
Squirrel Nutkin *69*, 71, 72, 145, 147
Stevenson, Robert Louis 124
Storey, Tom 116, 118, 137
The Story of a Fierce Bad Rabbit 83
Strangeways & Sons 65

Tabitha Twitchit 13, 88
The Tailor and Cutter 70
The Tailor of Gloucester 66–7, *68–71*, 124, 144
The Tale of Benjamin Bunny 60, 72, *73*, 73
The Tale of the Flopsy Bunnies 60, 88, 144
The Tale of Ginger and Pickles 60, 88–9, 101
The Tale of Jemima Puddle-Duck 82, *84*, 85, 138–40, *141*
The Tale of Johnny Town-Mouse 107, 108, *108*
The Tale of Kitty-in-Boots 61, 103
The Tale of Little Pig Robinson 21, 124
The Tale of Miss Moppet 83
The Tale of Mr Jeremy Fisher 49, 74, 83–5, *87*
The Tale of Mr Tod 60, 91, 101
The Tale of Mrs Tiggy-Winkle 74, 77, *77*, 78, 136, *140*, 141–2, *142–3*
The Tale of Mrs Tittlemouse 91
The Tale of Peter Rabbit 58–61, *58–60*, 62–8, 65, 79, 135, *144*, 145
The Tale of Pigling Bland 96, 98–101, *98–101*
The Tale of Samuel Whiskers 7, 86, *86*, 101
The Tale of Squirrel Nutkin 29, 57, *69*, 71, 74
The Tale of Timmy Tiptoes 91
The Tale of Tom Kitten 7, 85, *88*, 101

The Tale of Two Bad Mice 8, 73–4, *75*
The Tales of Beatrix Potter (ballet) 145
Tarn Hows 126–7, *126*, 128, 129
Tate Gallery, London 144
Taylor, Judy 145
Tenniel, Sir John *20*, 21
Thistleton-Dyer, Mr 54, 55–6
Thompson, Bruce 131
Thompson, Emma *60*, 61
The Times 104, 127
Tom Kitten 85, 86
Tom Kitten's Painting Book 107
Tom Thumb 73, 145
Tommy Brock 101
Troutbeck Park Farm 113–18, *114–15*, 127,
  149, 152
Tuppenny *121*, 122–3

Unitarians 17–19, 37, 52
United States of America 60, 61, 72,
  120–1, 124, 136

Vasconcellos, Josefina de 6, 13, 129, 131,
  136, 141
Victoria and Albert Museum, London
  146, 153

Wag-by-Wall 124
Wales 74, 78
Warne, Frederick 145
Warne, Frederick & Co. 41, 58, 59, 66–70,
  71, 72, 104, 106–9, 123, 124, 145
Warne, Fruing 74, 103, 106–9, 124
Warne, Harold 71, 77, 78, 90, 91, 98, 103,
  106–7
Warne, Millie 74, 79, 82–3, 85, 91, 94–5, 96
Warne, Norman *64*, 93, 94, 136
  friendship with Beatrix 68–70, 71, 74–5
  engagement to Beatrix 75–7, 98, 102

doll's house *75*
  death 78–9, 80
Warne, Winifred *75*, *77*, 78–9
Weatherly, Frederic E. 41
White, Gilbert 148
Windermere *32–3*, 91, 120, *120*
Woodward, Gertrude 65, 83, 96
Wordsworth, William 30
The World of Peter Rabbit and his Friends
  (films) 61, 145
World War I 102–3, 108
World War II 8, 16, 134–6
Wray Castle, Ambleside 30, *31*, 151, *151*

Yew Tree Farm 128–9, *128*

Zellweger, Renée 145–6, *147*

Picture Credits